# What Dogs Want

**Arden Moore**

# What Dogs Want

## A Visual Guide to Understanding
## Your Dog's Every Move

NEW
BURLINGTON
BOOKS

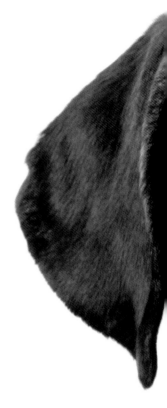

This edition first published in 2014 by
New Burlington Books:
The Old Brewery
6 Blundell Street
London N7 9BH

Quid Publishing
Level 4, Sheridan House
112-114 Western Road
Hove, BN3 1DD
United Kingdom
www.quidpublishing.com

10 9 8 7 6 5 4 3 2 1

A CIP catalogue record for this book is available from the British Library

ISBN 978-0-85762-332-4

Printed in China

Front cover: iStockphoto
Back cover: Shutterstock

# Contents

## 100 Postures, Expressions, Sounds, and Actions

# Behavior Types

# Foreword

*What Dogs Want* provides readers with a solid foundation for thoughtful and healthy relationships with their dogs, based on honest, clear communication—conveying intent, receiving the message, and responding accordingly. Accurate interpretations and representations of animal behavior are essential to humane communication. *What Dogs Want* does not shy away from the reality that dogs who coexist in a social setting must abide by some sort of hierarchical rules to maintain the peace. At the same time, it does not exaggerate or over-emphasize the importance of dominant and subordinate relationships.

*What Dogs Want* describes canine body language and vocalizations, then offers a variety of interpretations based on context. This is the great value of the book: the wide range of behavioral observations highlighted encourages readers to stop, look, and listen to what their dogs are trying to tell them. Pure, unadulterated communication always involves openly sharing and receiving, and is paramount for both people and their pets. Honest communication is an art, a science, and the basis for all good, meaningful relationships.

The primary goals of my animal behavior consultation practice are to teach people to understand the animal mind and to educate them on why their pets behave as they do. Equally vital is to teach people how they, themselves, can make their pets feel more secure and content, by assessing new situations and behavioral issues, and acting accordingly. The value of these skills cannot be overestimated.

I first met Arden Moore about 12 years ago in my role as a faculty member of the Animal Behavior Clinic at Tufts University's School of Veterinary Medicine, in Massachusetts. I was immediately impressed by her savvy communication skills and determination to deliver sound information on dog and cat care. She served as editor of *Catnip*, a national monthly affiliated with Tufts, and she was also a regular contributor to its canine publication, *Your Dog*. We worked closely together on every issue to make sure that readers of both publications received the best possible veterinary and behavioral advice.

Arden has gone on to become a best-selling author, animal behavior consultant, radio show host, in-demand professional speaker, and certified pet first-aid instructor. She has fine-tuned her animal-behavior observation and comprehension skills, and mastered her writing to bridge the communication gap between people and their pets—all of which is evident in the pages that follow.

**Alice Moon-Fanelli, PhD, CAAB,**
**Animal Behavior Consultations, LLC**

# Introduction

I happily share my home with two stellar communicators—a pair of rescued mutts who answer to the names of Chipper and Cleo. Although I am the one with the Bachelor's Degree in Communication from Purdue University, Indiana, Chipper and Cleo masterfully convey their wants and needs, rarely committing a communication miscue.

Their "talk" is always clear and consistent—whether they are communicating with me, each other, their canine pals, or even their feline housemates, Zeki and Murphy. Often, my dogs can convey their message without uttering a single sound. Their messages are delivered by their postures, tail positions, tail movements, eyes, expressions, actions, and much more. When Chipper turns her head and air snaps, then plops down with her rear end hoisted in the air, I know that she is ready for a friendly game of tug-of-war. When Cleo starts to pant and jumps onto my lap, I know that she needs to relieve her bladder outside.

Throughout my career, I have been both a student and a teacher of the art of communication. For two decades, I toiled as a reporter and editor for major daily newspapers. That profession taught me to speak less, listen more, and to observe body language so that I could better decipher whether people were telling the truth, hiding something, or embellishing the facts.

For the past dozen years, I have shifted my focus to studying and interpreting communication between pets and people. As an animal behavior consultant, host of the award-winning "Oh Behave!" show on Pet Life Radio, and author of 24 pet books, my goal is to narrow the communication gap between pets and their people, so everyone can enjoy greater harmony in the household. I founded Four Legged Life, an online pet community to help people "laugh, love, and learn" about their pets.

Dogs do their best to deliver their canine cues to us, but sometimes we misinterpret their signals. We may quickly declare a dog who spills his kibble on the kitchen floor to be a finicky, messy eater. But the real reason may be that he is enduring undiagnosed mouth pain because of a broken tooth or infected gum. We may not accurately distinguish the "bark-bark-bark" that our dog sounds to alert the approach of a delivery worker from the "bark-bark-bark" that he uses to convey sheer boredom and his need for purposeful play.

Help is here. The pages of *What Dogs Want* provide you with a visual guide that decodes 100 postures, expressions, sounds, and actions exhibited by dogs of all sizes, ages, and breeds. Paw through the pages and not only will you learn why your dog is acting or vocalizing in a specific manner, but you will also discover what you can do in response, to bring about his best behavior and health.

So, call your dog over, dive into these pages, and let clear communication between the two of you finally begin.

**Arden Moore**

# 1 Cowering

○   Your Great Dane suddenly shrinks to the size of a Beagle
    when a tall man with a booming voice rushes head-on to
    greet you and your dog.

○   Your dog backs up into a corner and lowers his body,
    doing his best to become invisible.

○   A shy dog takes on the "incredible shrinking dog"
    role when the canine boss of the local dog park
    trots over to do a body sniff.

○   Uh-oh, the fear factor has now crept
    into your dog's body, making him
    shake and quiver uncontrollably.

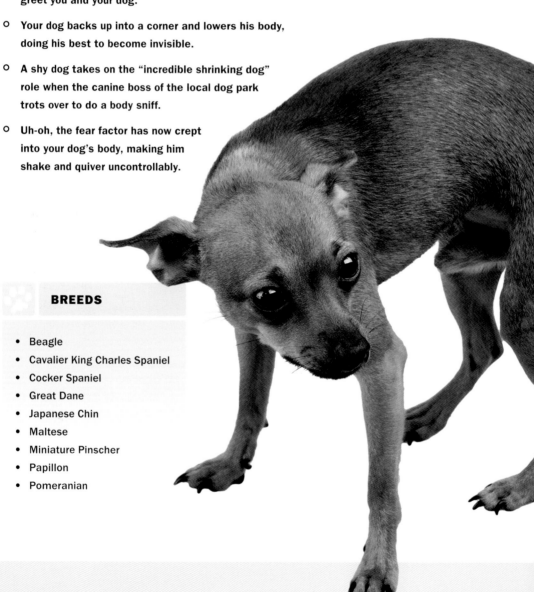

## BREEDS

- Beagle
- Cavalier King Charles Spaniel
- Cocker Spaniel
- Great Dane
- Japanese Chin
- Maltese
- Miniature Pinscher
- Papillon
- Pomeranian

## ? WHAT YOUR DOG WANTS

Submissive dogs have no qualms about being labeled cowards—but they stop short of sporting signs on their backs that read, "Bite me." They purposely make themselves small to communicate that they come in peace and pose absolutely no threat. It is the canine version of waving the white flag of surrender.

Some dogs cower because they have been victims of past physical abuse. These dogs skulk in order to protect themselves and to plead the case to leave them alone and unharmed.

Shrinking in size is also a sign of respect conveyed by a young pup toward a confident adult dog.

### VET'S NOTE

> Dogs can experience extreme anxiety or fear and some need more than kindness to improve. Certain dogs require calming prescriptive medication, coupled with behavior-modification training, in order to successfully become calm and feel more secure.

> Some dogs who cower may have been physically abused and should be given a full physical examination by a vet to detect any injuries to the body.

## ✓ HOW TO RESPOND

Dogs who cower are not crouching tigers of the canine world preparing for a hunt. They need a confidence boost. This can be accomplished by giving them a little time and space during initial introduction. When you see a dog crouch low, and perhaps lick his lips and avoid eye contact, sit down quietly on a chair or the floor a few feet away. Speak in a calm, upbeat tone and avoid making fast or exaggerated hand gestures.

Give this dog a chance to download you on his own time schedule. Try tossing a treat his way. If he does approach, let him sniff you. Do not reach your hand out over his head because the dog may perceive this as a threatening gesture and snap or bite you out of fear.

Dogs who cower need to develop dog socialization skills, too. Instead of forcing them to meet a pack of strange dogs at the local dog park, arrange a play date in a fenced backyard with a well-socialized dog, such as a therapy dog, for a little one-on-one, safe interaction.

# 2 Exposing Belly

○ Your dog looks like a hairy upside-down coffee table with all four legs hoisted up and swaying in the air.

○ Balancing on his back, your dog gains a unique perspective on everyone and everything in his view.

○ Faster than you can spell b-l-i-n-k, your dog flips over like a pancake on a hot griddle.

**BREEDS**

- Cocker Spaniel
- Golden Retriever
- Labrador Retriever

**WHAT YOUR DOG WANTS**

 **HOW TO RESPOND**

Most often, dogs strike this posture to garner love, attention, and perhaps a little assistance to scratch a hard-to-reach itch. They greet you with soft eyes and relaxed bodies.

However, check the whole canine package first before you bend down and offer a belly rub. Some cunning canines use this belly-up posture to lure in unsuspecting targets for bark, or even bite, attacks. Beware of dogs who make direct, hard stares and have tense bodies. These are not relaxed dogs waiting for TLC; they are setting a trap.

Some dogs drop, plop upside down, and make zero eye contact with a dog that is deemed higher-up in the canine hierarchy. By purposely exposing his vulnerable underbelly, this dog tells the dominant one that he has no intention of challenging his authority.

Sometimes a confident adult dog, secure in his surroundings, goes belly-up to get into a relaxed posture and even falls asleep like this.

Finally, there is less hair on the belly than elsewhere on a dog's body, so going belly-up is a great way to cool down on hot days and catch the breeze.

Happy dogs who belly-up at your feet the minute you walk in the door may be doing their best to let you know they have a lot of pent-up energy that needs to be unleashed. They adore you, and one way to show how much you adore them is by taking them out on a brisk, long walk. Give them time to stop and sniff and absorb all the great smells on your trek.

Fearful dogs who expose their bellies should not be pet as this may unintentionally trigger a fear-bite response. Speak to your fearful dog in upbeat tones, teach him how to shake paws, and reward him with a healthy treat while he is in the "sit" position.

Dominant dogs who strike this pose for selfish motives need to be reschooled in the basic cues of "sit," "stay," "watch me," and "down," to demote their status below that of yourself and other family members.

 **VET'S NOTE**

> *Inspect the belly and back, and look for prolonged wiggling. Your dog may be doing his best to fend off fleas.*
> *In rare instances, your dog may go belly-up before the start of a seizure caused by epilepsy or poisoning.*

# 3 Raising Hair on Back

○ The hair that runs along your dog's spine sprouts up in the blink of an eye.

○ Hmmm ... did my dog borrow my hair dryer?

○ Within seconds, your dog magically sports a canine Mohawk.

○ You are looking at the canine equivalent of human goose bumps.

## BREEDS

- Alaskan Malamute
- Rhodesian Ridgeback
- Siberian Husky
- Thai Ridgeback
- West Highland White Terrier

## WHAT YOUR DOG WANTS

When the hairs along a dog's back stand on end, it is called piloerection. This fight-or-flight response is a function of the sympathetic nervous system. It occurs because adrenalin causes certain muscles in the skin to contract and push up the hair follicles.

Fear and aggression are the most prevalent reasons why dogs raise their hackles. But dogs who are overly excited, aroused, or startled can also display piloerection.

Fearful dogs do this hair-raising act to bluff and look bigger and tougher, in the hope that an approaching dog will do an about-face and leave.

Dominant or aggressive dogs bristle hairs all along their backs as a clear sign that they plan to lunge and are prepared to use their teeth to attack.

Excited dogs raise their hackles when they smell a female in heat or spot a squirrel scurrying up a tree.

Some dogs, such as Rhodesian Ridgebacks and Thai Ridgebacks, are born with naturally raised hackles.

## HOW TO RESPOND

For a fearful dog, distract him by having him focus on an obedience cue, such as "sit" or "watch me." Do not pet or cuddle your dog, as this may cause him to be more fearful or to nip. Get to know his body language tendencies so that you can judge when to step in and prevent a fear state from surfacing.

For an aggressive or unknown dog who has raised hackles, avoid eye contact and back away slowly or stand still. Minimize movement to try to calm down this dog's prey drive. However, do not jump to conclusions that a dog is aggressive. Rhodesian Ridgebacks, for example, are born with naturally raised hackles. Study the dog's entire body language and survey the situation first to determine what emotions are really at play before you take action.

For a dog with hair that puffs up when he is exposed to cold temperatures, bring him inside or provide him with a dog coat or sweater for extra warmth.

If your dog is raising his hackles for no identified reason, consult your vet.

## VET'S NOTE

> *Piloerection can be a rare symptom of some brain tumors, temporal lobe epilepsy, and autonomic hyperreflexia.*

BEHAVIOR TYPES: **Aggressive** *p.178* • **Anxious/Stressed** *p.179* • **Dominant** *p.181* • **Fearful** *p.182* • **Playful** *p.183* • **Sexual** *p.185*

# 4 Resting Head on Paws

○ **If your dog could talk, he'd say, "patience may be a virtue, but I'm getting impatient waiting."**

○ **Without uttering a bark, your dog is saying he misses his canine housemate who passed away.**

## BREEDS

- **This posture is not limited to specific breeds.**

## VET'S NOTE

❯ *No specific medical advice for this posture.*

## WHAT YOUR DOG WANTS

When a dog is bored, he stretches his front legs, sighs, and slowly lowers his head to rest on top of his paws.

A dog who hopes to score a tidbit from your plate strikes this pose to look both forlorn and adorable. Or he is telling you he has grown ho-hum by being served the same kibble every day.

Some dogs make this pose to focus on what you are saying, ever hopeful that you will mention key favorite words, such as "treat" or "walk."

Dogs who miss their favorite people or canine friends strike this pose out of sadness.

## ✓ HOW TO RESPOND

Get active! Your dog is tired of not doing anything. He needs, and deserves, to try his mental and physical talents on learning a new trick or pawing out kibble from a dog-food puzzle.

He may spend too long in his crate or have limited room in a closed bathroom. Restrict your dog's crate time to no more than five or six hours at a stretch. Enroll him in an obedience class so he can develop good manners and be trusted to roam free in your home while you are at work.

Treat your sad dog to a therapeutic massage or a walk in a new place to help shake the dog glooms.

BEHAVIOR TYPES: **Attention-seeking** *p.179* • **Bored** *p.180* • **Sad** *p.184*

# 5 Circular Tail Wagging

- This movement resembles a hairy windmill on a breezy day.

- The wag is often matched with an open grin, squinty eyes, flat ears, and a relaxed or swaying body.

### VET'S NOTE

> No specific medical advice for this posture.

### BREEDS

- Belgian Tervuren
- Boxer
- Cardigan Welsh Corgi
- Collie
- Doberman Pinscher
- German Shepherd
- Golden Retriever
- Keeshond
- Labrador Retriever
- Rottweiler

### WHAT YOUR DOG WANTS

This is one happy, friendly dog, eager to greet you, play with you, or romp with his favorite canine pal.

Breeds with long, bushy tails, such as the Belgian Tervuren and Keeshond, are not shy about showing affection to their favorite people.

Breeds with stubby tails, such as Boxers and Rottweilers, cause their tails to appear to vibrate and wiggle their whole bodies, or prance on their hind legs, to show their excitement.

### HOW TO RESPOND

Your gleeful dog is begging to interact with you in a fun way. Try a little canine cha-cha or exchange high fives from hand to paw.

Athletic dogs involved in sports, such as dock diving or agility, unleash circular wags as they wait for their chance to take center stage. Use this time to calm your dog down and get him focused on you, so he does not become overexcited.

A dog wags his tail in a circular motion as a signal to other dogs that he wants to play. This is reinforced with play bows. To encourage play, maintain an open posture and speak in an upbeat tone.

BEHAVIOR TYPES: Attention-seeking p.179 • Confident p.180 • Happy p.182 • Playful p.183

# 6 Stiff Tail Wagging

○ The tail is parallel to the ground or straight up, and moves slowly but powerfully from side to side.

○ The face joins the tail in this "I-mean-business" posture, with tight muscles and a steady, unblinking stare.

○ The back legs are wide apart and rigid, and your dog is leaning forward.

## BREEDS

- Airedale
- Alaskan Malamute
- Basenji
- Boxer
- Bulldog
- Dalmatian
- Doberman Pinscher
- German Shepherd
- Shar Pei
- Siberian Husky

## WHAT YOUR DOG WANTS

Tail-speak is clear and candid, and is never deceptive. Your dog is declaring to others to keep their distance when he strikes a tense body pose and stiffens and slows his tail movement to mimic the beat of a metronome. If you or another dog invades his perceived safety zone, he will snarl, lunge, and may even lash out.

A confident, alert dog hoists his tail up and makes slow side-to-side sweeps as he focuses on a situation and decides how he is going to act and react.

This tail posture signals high-ranking status in the dog world. A dominant dog wags his tail stiffly and slowly when he is being approached or when he confronts another dog. In response, the lower-ranked dog usually avoids direct eye contact and lowers his tail. Sometimes lower-ranked dogs even tuck their tails as a sign of submission to dominant dogs.

Different dog breeds carry their tails at different heights, but in general dogs who are concerned, focused, and ready to go into attack mode keep their tails stiff and parallel to the ground or raised. Some breeds that have curled tails, such as the Basenji, increase the tightness in their tails in these scenarios.

## HOW TO RESPOND

Heed the dog's message not to engage. Do not rush in to try to pet a dog who is still sizing you and the situation up, and deciding whether to stay and fight or to flee. Do not stare directly into his eyes because he will perceive this action as threatening.

Look at the dog's entire body posture, especially in dogs with cropped or docked tails, such as Doberman Pinschers, Boxers, and Bulldogs.

Toss a treat to a weary dog when he makes this posture, to try to shift his mood from cautious to calm. Do not attempt to hand-feed this dog or you may get bit.

## VET'S NOTE

> Check your dog's tail if he is normally a happy tail-wagger and has suddenly slowed his tempo. He may have an injury to his tail that requires a vet's attention.
> Dogs that are aggressive need behavior-modification training and, possibly, prescription medications from a vet behaviorist or certified-applied animal behaviorist. Training a dog from being in fight mode to acceptance takes time and professional intervention.

BEHAVIOR TYPES: Aggressive p.178 • Confident p.180 • Dominant p.181 • Predatory p.184

# 7 Play Bow

○ A happy dog plops down with his front legs extended, his shoulders and chest low to the ground, and his rear end pushed up in the air.

○ Your dog brings out his goofy best in the hope that you will join in for playtime.

○ This is the universal "let's play" sign for dogs of all sizes, ages, breeds, and social rankings.

## BREEDS

• This posture is not limited to specific breeds.

## WHAT YOUR DOG WANTS

One of the most delightful canine postures is the play bow. As its name implies, this is the official extend-the-party invitation in the canine world.

Some dogs add a play smile to this pose by pulling their lips back horizontally, but they do not bare their teeth, which could be mistaken for a sign of aggression.

The beauty of the play bow is that social hierarchy is not a factor. Dominant dogs can offer play bows to lower-ranked dogs and vice versa. When two dogs meet for the first time, they may get into play bows.

Dogs have a keen sense of humor and are always up for a playful romp with their favorite canine pals. In true play mode, dogs may play rough but they do their best to communicate actions that are anything but threatening. Dogs may switch off making play bows, or one will immediately go into a play-bow posture after accidentally body slamming his playmate too roughly. In this case, the play bow is used to say, "Oops, I'm sorry. Let's keep playing."

Sometimes as part of the mating ritual, a dog will initially assume the play-bow position to communicate a friendly gesture. A male may make play bows to win over an aloof female in heat.

## HOW TO RESPOND

Okay, so you are no canine, but you can get your dog in a playful mood by plopping into a play bow yourself. Sport your goofiest expression, unleash some happy talk, and watch your dog shift from bored to elated in nanoseconds. You can also get down on the floor and whisper to your dog—this is regarded as the canine equivalent to human laughter.

Purposeful play is important to your dog's overall well-being. When he offers you a play bow, treat the both of you to even just five minutes of playful interaction. Take a break from your "must-do" list and revel in the moment with your canine chum. Pick an activity he really craves, such as fetch, tug-of-war, or racing back and forth in the backyard together.

Dogs who lack proper socialization may not know how to respond to another dog's play-bow invitation. They may feel threatened and growl in fear. Work with a professional dog trainer to improve this dog's social skills.

## VET'S NOTE

> *No specific medical advice for this posture.*

BEHAVIOR TYPES: **Attention-seeking** *p.179* • **Happy** *p.182* • **Playful** *p.183* • **Sexual** *p.185*

# 8 Raising Front Paw

- From this posture, a dog can do the wave, give you a high five, or touch his favorite person.

- Your dog may be telling you, "I just spotted a bird and I am showing you that he is right over there."

- Or he may be conveying, "Look ma, I can balance on three legs."

- Your dog may have stepped on something that is causing pain to his paw.

- Savvy dogs know this is a quick and cute way to get attention—pronto.

## BREEDS

- Beagle
- Bichon Frise
- Border Collie
- Boxer
- Chesapeake Bay Retriever
- English Springer Spaniel
- German Shorthaired Pointer
- Jack (Parson) Russell Terrier
- Labrador Retriever
- Poodle

## WHAT YOUR DOG WANTS

By tactfully lifting a front paw and staring at you with sweet eyes, your dog can accomplish his single-minded mission—to get you to stop what you are doing and fulfill his wish for treats, play, or other desires.

Certain hunting breeds, such as Beagles and German Shorthaired Pointers, are trained to stand still and raise a front paw to point out where game is for hunters.

Ouch! Dogs in pain because of injuries caused by stepping on a sharp object, catching a foxtail or spur between the toes, or straining a leg muscle, will do their best to take weight off that leg.

When your dog is in a new place or meeting a dog or person for the first time, he may lift a front paw because he feels uneasy.

Young, nursing puppies raise a paw in response to being licked by their mothers.

## VET'S NOTE

> Curious to a fault, a dog can paw at a beehive and be stung, or step on an anthill. Insect bites can cause swelling and irritation to paws and in between toes, and may need medication to treat.
> One miscued motion or a leap from too high a place can cause injury to your dog's front leg or paw. A vet will need to examine and treat the injury with medication and possibly surgery.

## HOW TO RESPOND

Be careful not to let your fast-growing puppy learn to train you. Sure, it is a cute gesture when a young dog lifts his front paw toward you and earns petting or a treat. But if you comply with each request, he will learn to do it more frequently and with greater insistence.

Ignore the paw by standing up and leaving the room. Or have your dog do another action, such as "come" on command. Reward him for coming to you, not for the raised paw.

Regularly feel your dog's paws so that he gets used to having them touched. Inspect his paws after hikes and long walks to make sure the paw pad is not injured and there are no foreign objects, such as burrs, stuck in between his toes.

BEHAVIOR TYPES: **Affectionate** p.178 • **Anxious/Stressed** p.179 • **Attention-seeking** p.179 • **Bored** p.180 • **Curious** p.181 • **Playful** p.183

# 9 Chasing Tail

○ It is easy to get dizzy watching a dog go round and round as he attempts to grab his own tail.

○ Even the dog does not know if he is coming or going.

○ Most dogs chase their tails by running in either clockwise or counterclockwise directions.

○ The tail usually moves just fast enough to avoid being snagged in the dog's mouth.

### VET'S NOTE

❯ *When a dog catches his tail in his mouth, he can be in high prey-drive mode and bite down, causing bleeding. Apply pressure to prevent blood loss and make sure a vet treats the wound.*

❯ *A dog who makes this posture may be suffering from an irritated anal sac.*

❯ *Medications to treat obsessive-compulsive disorders may be needed in cases where dogs spin excessively. These dogs may lose weight because they lose interest in eating and fail to get adequate sleep.*

❯ *Untreated, excessive chewing could result in surgical amputation of the tail.*

## WHAT YOUR DOG WANTS

The reasons that dogs chase their tails range from the simple, "because I can," to the serious case of obsessive-compulsiveness. Other dogs engage in tail pursuit because of a prey drive. They are startled when they spot something moving, or more accurately, wagging, out of the corner of their eye and give chase.

However, the most common reason for tail chasing is boredom. Some dogs sit alone at home for hours with nothing to do but take yet another nap. They look for an outlet for nervous, pent-up energy.

Other dogs feel frustrated that they cannot stalk real prey, such as chasing birds or squirrels, and they take it out on their poor tails, literally.

Puppies chase their tails for fun, but a healthy dog should outgrow this behavior by the time he is an adult.

### BREEDS

- Australian Cattle Dog
- Bull Terrier
- German Shepherd
- Italian Greyhound
- Jack (Parson) Russell Terrier
- Pug
- Whippet

## HOW TO RESPOND

Bored dogs who chase their tails need constructed activity. Hire a professional dog walker or take your dog along to a dog daycare center a few times a week to give him opportunities to exercise and interact with other dogs.

Provide your dog with different keep-busy toys while you are gone. Stuff a hard-rubber chew toy with kibble or cheese, which a dog then works at to get out.

Initially and in mild stages, this posture may appear cute and you may laugh, which will only reinforce your dog's actions. Be careful not to encourage him or give in to his plea for attention. Clap your hands to disrupt the movement and redirect your dog to an appropriate activity, such as fetching a ball.

If he suddenly starts circling, stop your dog and inspect his tail carefully. He may have fleas or a skin rash and need treatment by a vet. New studies report a link between tail chasing and high cholesterol levels, and are yet another reason to take your tail-chasing dog to a vet.

BEHAVIOR TYPES: Anxious/Stressed p.179 • Bored p.180 • Curious p.181 • Obsessive-Compulsive p.183 • Playful p.183 • Predatory p.184

# 10 Tail Tucked Under

- Poof! One minute your dog's tail is hoisted high, and the next it seems to have vanished in thin air.

- Frightened dogs will tolerate being uncomfortable by resting their bodies on their tail squished between their hind legs.

## BREEDS

- This posture is not limited to specific breeds.

## WHAT YOUR DOG WANTS

No butt sniffing, please. By tucking his tail between his back legs or sitting down, your unsure dog is doing his best to prevent an approaching strange dog from sniffing out how scared he is. The scent glands do not lie—they convey a dog's true state of mind.

Dogs also use this tail-tuck, sit-down maneuver in self-defense, to prevent another dog from mounting them and trying to engage in sexual intercourse.

Timid, lower-ranking dogs and young pups show respect to higher-ranking dogs by tucking their tails. This stance clearly shows that they pose absolutely not a hint of trouble. Small dogs often bow to larger dogs by tucking their tails during the dog meet-and-greet.

## VET'S NOTE

> *Easily frightened dogs, unable to cope with thunderstorms or other noise phobias, may need to be prescribed antianxiety medications by a vet.*
> *If you breed your female dog, prevent potential male suitors from getting close to her while she is in heat by keeping her indoors or on a leash in fenced outdoor areas.*

## HOW TO RESPOND

Recognize the triggers that cause fright or stress in your dog. Bail him out by doing your best not to expose him to these fearful encounters. For example, if your dog tucks his tail every time he sees and hears a skateboard, avoid taking him on a walk that passes the skateboard park.

Do not speak in a cooing voice to your frightened dog, as it will only worsen his fear. Do not yell at him, either, or force him to come face-to-face with the object of his fear. This will just cause him to shut down emotionally.

When you walk your dog, switch to the other side of the street if you see another dog heading in your direction that is yanking on his leash and walking swiftly ahead of his owner. This is clearly a confident and possibly dominant dog looking to boost his ego. Avoid a likely introduction that will only increase feelings of stress and anxiety in your dog. As you move out of the way, cue your dog to "watch me" and have him "sit" or "shake paws"—simple requests that will distract him and boost his confidence. And be sure to reward him with a healthy treat.

Try to introduce your dog to other well-socialized dogs who pose no threat to him during play. These canine pals will teach him essential dog etiquette.

BEHAVIOR TYPES: **Anxious/Stressed** *p.179* • **Fearful** *p.182* • **Sexual** *p.185* • **Submissive** *p.185*

# 11 Walking on Hind Legs

- With the grace of a ballerina, your dog places all his weight on his hind legs as he steps forward.

- Some talented dogs can balance on their back legs and circle or hop forward and backward.

- A small dog can suddenly soar to twice his height by standing on his hind legs.

## BREEDS

- Bichon Frise
- Chihuahua
- Japanese Chin
- Miniature Pinscher
- Papillon
- Poodle
- Yorkshire Terrier

## WHAT YOUR DOG WANTS

Some dogs are born performers and do what they can to capture your attention and applause—in the form of treats, of course. They revel in being showered with praise, and it motivates them to keep performing. It makes them feel special.

Small and medium-sized breeds with long legs and lean bodies are best suited to hoisting up their upper bodies and maintaining balance while walking on their back legs. They are often the daredevils of the dog world, open to trying new challenges.

Dogs with front-leg injuries or diseases, such as osteosarcoma, show their adaptive abilities and will to survive by shifting their weight to their back legs to move. Some senior dogs may develop arthritis in their front legs, which causes them to favor their hind legs.

## VET'S NOTE

> *Anti-inflammatory medications may be necessary to help a dog who has temporarily lost the ability to put weight on his front legs.*
> *Spinal injuries, as well as neurological disorders, can impede a dog from placing weight on his front legs. Surgery may be necessary.*
> *Some dogs can be fitted for dogcarts to adequately support their body weight and enable them to maintain mobility.*

## HOW TO RESPOND

If an attention-seeking canine attempts this posture, grab a pile of small treats and your clicker so you can accurately shape the action. The goal of the clicker is to deliver a distinctive sound to your dog to confirm what he just did is what you wanted. It is called "marking the behavior."

To train a healthy, athletic dog to consistently walk on his hind legs, first teach him to sit up. Next, get him to master holding a begging position. Now you are ready to get him to shift to the stand-up position on his hind legs. Face your dog at eye level and using a treat by your eye, slowly rise up and encourage your dog to move up with you. Click when he does and give him the treat. Be patient and build on all small successes along the way.

If your dog becomes bossy by prancing in front of you all of the time, ignore him and walk away. Do not say anything, as you will unintentionally give him what he was seeking—attention.

BEHAVIOR TYPES: **Affectionate** *p.178* • **Attention-seeking** *p.179* • **Happy** *p.182* • **Playful** *p.183*

# 12 Rubbing against Furniture

○ Who needs furniture polish when your dog sports a large, fluffy tail?

○ That dark smudge on your beige-colored sofa has bits of dog hair protruding from it.

## BREEDS

• This posture is not limited to specific breeds.

## WHAT YOUR DOG WANTS

Leaving his scent on your furniture is a dog's way of telling others that this sofa belongs to him. It is an obvious turf-claiming action.

He may also lack the ability to reach an itchy spot on his body, caused by dry skin, allergies, or fleas. The recliner arm or the corner of the coffee table may have just the right configuration to ease your dog's itch.

Some dogs regard fabric-covered furniture as giant napkins for them to wipe their faces and muzzles to rid food particles after mealtimes.

## VET'S NOTE

❭ *If your dog persistently scratches and rubs against furniture, look for evidence of fleas. Your vet can recommend the appropriate flea-fighting medication.*

## HOW TO RESPOND

Look for a pattern as to when and how your dog rubs against furniture to pinpoint the cause. Inspect his coat for signs of fleabites or skin allergies. Maintain the monthly flea treatment and consult your vet about switching your dog to a different diet if he has food allergies.

If your dog wants to wipe his face after a meal, have a slightly wet hand towel ready and give his face a good clean before you allow him to race into the living room.

BEHAVIOR TYPES: Anxious/Stressed *p.179* • Attention-seeking *p.179* • Bored *p.180* • Dominant *p.181* • Happy *p.182* • Playful *p.183*

# 13 Raised Tail

- The tail is upright and rigid.

- The body stiffens and becomes motionless.

- The hair may bristle and rise along your dog's spine to make him appear bigger.

## BREEDS

- American Foxhound
- Beagle
- Catahoula Leopard
- Coonhound
- English Foxhound
- Siberian Husky
- Tibetan Spaniel

## VET'S NOTE

› *No specific medical advice for this posture.*

## ? WHAT YOUR DOG WANTS

The raised tail is a yellow caution light. In most cases, a dog hoists his tail straight up to assert his authority over another dog. As the dog's attitude shifts from cautionary to more dominant, or even anger, his tail goes almost rigid.

Hunting breeds, such as Beagles and American Foxhounds, raise their tails to show the white tip to hunters when they have spotted birds or other game. Confident, friendly dogs raise their tails to expose their anal area, allowing other dogs to more easily sniff during greetings. Female dogs in heat will raise their tails to beckon male suitors.

## ✓ HOW TO RESPOND

Clear communication is a hallmark of canine body language and the position and motion, or lack of, in the tail is key.

Some dogs are less able to rely on tail-speak because they have tails that are held close to their rumps or that are small and tightly curled. For these dogs, you need to pay close attention to their entire stance.

Move your dog on the leash to break its steady stare at another dog. Have him heed a cue to reinforce your authority.

BEHAVIOR TYPES: **Aggressive** *p.178* • **Confident** *p.180* • **Curious** *p.181* • **Dominant** *p.181* • **Sexual** *p.185*

# 14 Twitching while Sleeping

- Your snoozing dog suddenly starts moving his feet but his eyes stay closed.

- His body starts to twitch and quiver and he may vocalize a little.

- Your dog looks like he is running on his side.

- The twitch can be sporadic, starting and stopping for a few seconds or longer.

## BREEDS

- Beagle
- Bull Mastiff
- Collie
- Dogue de Bordeaux
- French Mastiff
- Golden Retriever
- Keeshond
- Labrador Retriever
- Poodle

### VET'S NOTE

> If you are unsure whether your dog is a deep dreamer or suffering a seizure, have your vet give him a complete physical examination. Any dog can develop seizures, but some are more genetically predisposed.

> If your dog looks like he is trying to chew his tongue and you detect pulsing between his eyes and temple, these could be signs that he has been infected with distemper. It is important that you maintain your dog's vaccinations.

> Persistent leg twitching at night could signal nerve damage or even muscular dystrophy.

## WHAT YOUR DOG WANTS

Just like us, dogs dream. They go through three sleep stages: NREM, non-rapid eye movement; REM, rapid-eye movement; and SWS, short-wave sleep. It is in the SWS stage that a dog breathes heavily while he is sleeping. Animal experts theorize that dogs dream during the REM stage, and act on their dreams by twitching or moving all four paws as if they were chasing a rabbit.

Dogs who sleep all curled up must keep their muscles tensed and are therefore less relaxed than dogs who stretch out when they sleep.

For reasons yet to be explained, young puppies and senior dogs both tend to move more in their sleep and to dream more than adult dogs. If you are sleeping close by, these dogs may unintentionally wake you up because of their jerky body movements.

## HOW TO RESPOND

Do not panic when you see your sleeping dog start to twitch. Gently call out his name to wake him. Some dogs can be touchy and reactive while sleeping, so do not use your hand to rouse them or you may get bit. For your safety, honor that adage: "let sleeping dogs lie."

Some dogs have nightmares and wake up frightened. Speak to these dogs calmly to reassure them when they wake.

Dips in temperature can cause cold dogs to twitch while sleeping, in the body's attempt to stay warm. Turn up the heat or provide your dog with a blanket.

Know the difference between benign dreamland twitching and a seizure. During sleep twitching, your dog may make a jerky movement or two, but he will fall back to a quiet sleep. If you call his name, he will wake up. During a seizure, your dog's body is stiff, trembles heavily, and may lock up. He can lose consciousness and may pant excessively. He will not respond to his name being called.

BEHAVIOR TYPES: **Anxious/Stressed** p.179 • **Playful** p.183 • **Predatory** p.184

# 15 Flattening Ears

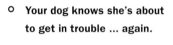

○ Both ears are pulled tight against the head.

○ Brow and skull muscles may be tight and tense.

○ Mouth may be open and relaxed, or stiffly closed.

○ The ears are folded back and out, like the wings of an airplane.

○ Your dog knows she's about to get in trouble ... again.

## BREEDS

• This expression is not limited to specific breeds.

## VET'S NOTE

❯ Certain long-eared breeds, including Cocker Spaniels, Cavalier King Charles Spaniels, Poodles, and Saint Bernards, need regular grooming and ear inspection because they grow hair in their ears that can lead to earwax buildup and infections.

**WHAT YOUR DOG WANTS**

 **HOW TO RESPOND**

To truly deduce a dog's mood, you need to see beyond flattened ears. Dogs on different ends of the emotional spectrum—from fearful to aggressive—flatten their ears, so look for the following distinct differences:

· A fearful dog sports a smooth forehead and cowers;

· An aggressive dog's forehead is tense and wrinkled and she may draw her lips back to show a snarl;

· A curious dog pulls her ears back in concentration;

· A sad dog lays her head on her front paws with her ears back, and usually lies motionless.

Just before a fight, dogs flatten their ears to protect them from being bit or scratched by paws.

When greeting upset owners after having urinated or defecated in the house, dogs usually project a submissive posture, which includes flattening the ears. This is a dog's way of conveying that she recognizes her lower ranking in the household hierarchy.

It is difficult for breeds that have long, heavy ears, such as Beagles and Basset Hounds, to flatten their ears and communicate they are submissive and non-threatening. Breeds with erect, triangular ears, such as German Shepherds or Cairn Terriers, are able to get this message across more clearly.

A dog who has an ear infection may flatten her ears and lean her head to one side because of the itchiness or irritation.

Some dogs push their ears back when they feel uncertain, such as when their nails are being trimmed.

You may feel frustrated or angry when your dog does something naughty, such as making a house-soiling mess, but yelling at her will not stop this unwanted action. Instead, it may backfire and cause your dog to be more submissive and fearful around you. The best thing to do is to usher her outside and praise her when she performs her bathroom duties in the right place.

Regularly inspect your dog's ears and sniff inside them to catch any medical problem early, especially if she flattens and rubs them. Also check for any burrs or foxtails that may have lodged in your dog's ears after you return from a hike.

Be careful when you approach a fearful dog who has her ears back, her tail tucked, and her body lowered. A dog in this state may believe her only recourse to your advance is to nip and flee.

BEHAVIOR TYPES: **Aggressive** p.178 · **Anxious/Stressed** p.179 · **Curious** p.181 · **Fearful** p.182 · **Submissive** p.185

# 16 Cupping Ears

○ **When the ears are up, the head leans forward or to one side.**

○ **Both ears are up and forward and the eyes are alert and focused.**

## BREEDS

• **This expression is not limited to specific breeds.**

## VET'S NOTE

❯ *No specific medical advice for this expression.*

## WHAT YOUR DOG WANTS

Ready-for-play canines arch their ears up and forward when they see something of great interest, such as a person picking up a tennis ball. They are excited and getting ready for playtime.

Curious dogs cup their ears when watching animals on a high-definition television screen. They are trying to figure out whether or not the animals, which appear one-dimensional and do not emit odors, are real.

Confident, alert dogs raise their ears forward and cast a steady, though not intense, stare. This conveys that they feel strong and secure in their surroundings.

When hunting dogs spot prey, they focus intently, hoist their ears, and open their mouths slightly.

## ✓ HOW TO RESPOND

Pay heed when your dog cups her ears and looks intently—she may be tuning into an unwanted critter in your backyard, such as a raccoon or possum. Or she may be ready to announce that someone is approaching the front door.

Gauge the amount of tension in her ears. Prey-minded or aggressive dogs display more tension than playful, curious, or alert dogs.

BEHAVIOR TYPES: **Aggressive** *p.178* • **Confident** *p.180* • **Curious** *p.181* • **Playful** *p.183* • **Predatory** *p.184*

# 17 Eyebrow Raising

- One or both eyebrows raised with wide eyes showing white.

- Your dog is in a sit posture, ready to spring up on all four legs.

## BREEDS

- This expression is not limited to specific breeds.

## VET'S NOTE

› *No specific medical advice for this expression.*

## WHAT YOUR DOG WANTS

Dogs taken by surprise—in a good way, such as when being presented with a grade-A level treat—may raise their eyebrows and widen their eyes in astonishment. Think of this as the canine version of a person walking into their home on their birthday and having friends shout out, "Surprise!"

Unsure about what is going to happen next, an anxious dog may raise her eyebrows and close her mouth as she studies her surroundings.

A pair of dogs in play may raise their eyebrows in response to one another's actions. For example, one dog may raise her eyebrows in admiration when her play pal snags a flying object at a full run and leap.

## ✓ HOW TO RESPOND

This dog is living in the moment, not thinking about the past or fretting about the future. She serves as a gentle reminder that we need to put away our cell phones, move away from the computer keyboard, and play with our dogs—even for just five minutes a day.

Take advantage of your dog when she is in this alert mindset and teach her a new trick. Practice in a place with no distractions and be sure to heap on the praise and treats.

BEHAVIOR TYPES: **Anxious/Stressed** *p.179* • **Attention-seeking** *p.179* • **Curious** *p.181* • **Happy** *p.182*

# 18 Staring Intensely

○  No blinking or eye movement can be detected.

○  The head leans forward and the body is still.

○  The mouth is usually shut.

○  The eyes appear larger than normal.

### BREEDS

• This expression is not limited to specific breeds.

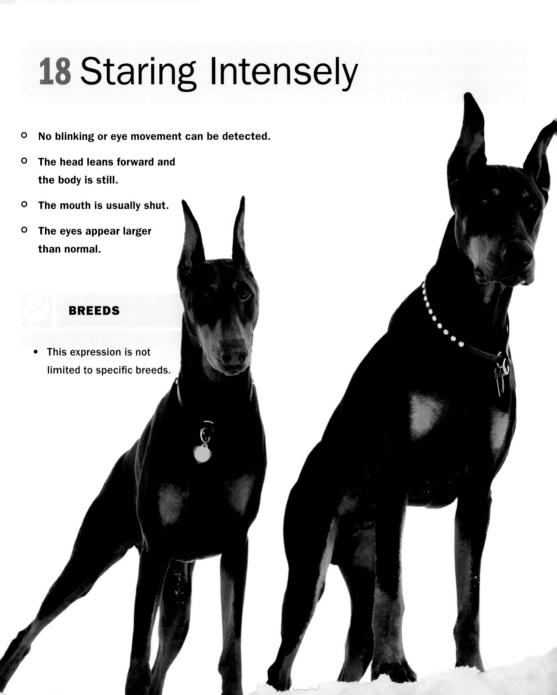

## WHAT YOUR DOG WANTS

What is more powerful and more frightening than barking? Casting a cold, hard stare without uttering a sound. When assessing a perceived lower-ranking dog, a confident, dominant dog engages in a steady stare to show her higher status. With that look, she tells the other dog not to even think about challenging her.

A confident dog will make eye contact with another dog while going into a play bow, or even roll over onto her back to show she is not a coward.

Not all staring is based on dominance. Some dogs are masters at staring and aim their non-blinking gaze at people at the dinner table in the hope of wearing them down enough to score a table scrap.

Other dogs combine staring with standing by the door to communicate that they want to go for a walk.

Dogs obsessed with playing fetch may stare at a tennis ball on the ground with great intensity until you pick it up and toss it for them.

If your dog has been exposed to poison, distemper, or suffers from a neurological condition, she may look vacantly into space. Her pupils may not react to movement and may be dilated.

## VET'S NOTE

> If your dog acts lethargic or is non-responsive and stares with a blank look on her face, she may have suffered a head trauma, swallowed poison, slipped into shock, or be suffering from another serious medical condition that warrants immediate vet care.

 ## HOW TO RESPOND

When you meet a dog of unknown temperament, it is okay to look at her but do not hold your gaze because she may misinterpret it as a threat and strike a ready-to-attack posture. Instead, lower your eyes or look away after making initial eye contact to convey that you are not a threat.

Try clapping your hands or whistling to break up a stare-down between your dog and another, and to stop both dogs' emotions from escalating.

To prevent your dog from demanding you play fetch, and for how long, have her get into a "sit" position between ball or object tosses. When you are ready to end the game, take the ball/object and put it out of reach and sight of your dog.

Usher your dog into another room before you sit down for a meal, to prevent her from being a successful food beggar. Time her mealtime so that it is in synch with yours. This way, she will be busy eating in the other room while you enjoy your meal in peace.

BEHAVIOR TYPES: **Aggressive** *p.178* • **Curious** *p.181* • **Dominant** *p.181* • **Obsessive-Compulsive** *p.183* • **Predatory** *p.184*

# 19 Head Bowing

o   Your dog's head is low with eyes looking up at you.

o   This is the dog equivalent of waiting for a courtroom verdict.

o   Dogs with giant eyes and large, wrinkled foreheads deliver the best hangdog looks.

### BREEDS

- Basset Hound
- Beagle
- Bloodhound
- English Foxhound

## WHAT YOUR DOG WANTS

Some dogs bow their heads to avoid a fight. In a two-dog household, the higher-ranking dog who wants to enforce the household rules may stare, bare teeth, and wrinkle her nose at the lower-ranking dog to get her to drop a chew toy from her mouth. The canine "thief" will lower her head and body in compliance to the higher-ranking dog as an act of submission.

Dogs can get the blues. A dog may lower her head as if to sigh as she watches her favorite person grab a suitcase and head out the door to go on a long trip or off to college. This astute canine knows suitcases signify separation from beloved people.

Submissive, shy, or anxious dogs who are unsure of how a person will react to them may drop their heads and look up slightly. This expression is similar to one some accused people make when a judge is about to read the verdict that proclaims them innocent or guilty. Dogs—and people—who make the hangdog look are feeling apprehensive about what is going to happen next.

If a dog is trapped in a corner with no escape in sight, she braces herself for the worst by lowering her head and staring at the approaching person or dog. This is a fear-dominated posture that may lead to the dog lunging, growling, and even attacking as a way to protect herself.

## HOW TO RESPOND

For starters, think more like a dog. Scrap the misguided notion that dogs feel guilt, an emotion that seems reserved for the human species alone.

The following is a classic case of misinterpretation: your home-alone dog chewed a house slipper into confetti or piddled on the living-room carpet. Five hours later, you return home to discover the mess and scold your dog. She strikes a submissive pose—her head is lowered, her eyes peer up at you, and her tail is tucked. You take this as a sign that your dog is sorry for what she has done and is telling you she will not do it again.

Wrong! Your dog is not apologizing for her bad deed but, rather, she is reacting to your voice tone, body language, and emotions. She hangs her head as a way of regaining favor with her pack leader—you—and to show that she is ready to do what she can to please you.

## VET'S NOTE

> *Some dogs with abdominal pain or stomach upset lower their heads and may even vomit. If there is any blood or a foreign object in the vomit, contact your vet immediately.*

BEHAVIOR TYPES: **Attention-seeking** *p.179* • **Fearful** *p.182* • **Sad** *p.184* • **Submissive** *p.185*

# 20 Squinting Eyes

○  The eyes are soft and half-open,
   the mouth is open and you almost
   detect a smile.

○  The eyes squint, the front paw is
   slightly raised, and the relaxed
   tail sweeps gently back and forth.

○  While receiving a relaxing belly rub,
   your dog's eyes communicate pure
   canine bliss.

○  After a ride in the car, your dog
   makes a mental note to stop
   sticking her head out of the
   window because specks
   fly into her eyes. Ouch!

## BREEDS

•  This expression is not
   limited to specific breeds.

## WHAT YOUR DOG WANTS

Dogs use their eyes to convey moods, and top of the squint list is canine contentment. Happy dogs narrow their eyes or half-close them when they feel blissful and safe. Body muscles are relaxed, as if on vacation.

Just like us, canine eyes are no match for the mighty sun, and when dogs stare into sunlight, the intensity of the sun's rays causes them to squint.

During a dog-to-dog introduction, a confident, socialized dog will squint and slightly divert her gaze to indicate that she is not at all interested in a bark-off or canine fight.

After being scolded by her owners for digging in the trash or performing other misdeeds, a dog may squint and gently nose a person's hand for forgiveness. She hates being in the "emotional" doghouse.

If your dog is angered by a rude dog or feels the need to defend herself, she may narrow her eyes as she follows every step the other dog makes.

## VET'S NOTE

> Prolonged squinting is not normal behavior. Your dog may have an eye infection, a scratched cornea, or debris on her eye. Vet care is warranted if she paws her eyes, holds one or both closed, tears excessively, discharges pus, or repeatedly rubs her face.

> An inquisitive dog uses her nose and front paws to investigate. If a bee or hornet has stung your curious dog, she needs antihistamine to reduce the swelling. Consult your vet for the proper dosage.

## HOW TO RESPOND

Tune into your dog's mood and treat her to a head-to-tail massage. This will improve circulation and blood flow.

Pet-proof your home to reduce the chance of your dog behaving like a canine "Dennis the Menace." Stash the kitchen trash can out of reach and make sure it has a sturdy lid. This will prevent her from making a mess and squinting at you when discovered, as an act of submission.

A side effect of some eye diseases is light sensitivity through to a condition known as photophobia. Dogs who suffer from such conditions must avoid bright sunlight and may need to be fitted with dog goggles or special canine sunglasses.

Do not let your dog stick her head out of an open window while she is riding in a vehicle. Secure her in a carrier or canine seatbelt restraint to keep her safe. This will minimize the chance of flying debris getting into her eye. Restraining your dog also allows you to drive without canine distractions.

BEHAVIOR TYPES: **Affectionate** p.178 • **Aggressive** p.178 • **Confident** p.180 • **Fearful** p.182 • **Happy** p.182 • **Submissive** p.185

# 21 Glancing Sideways

○ **Your dog's head is turned and she looks out of the corners of her eyes.**

○ **A play-seeking dog has a relaxed face and her mouth is open.**

○ **Your dog takes a peek at you—then looks away.**

## VET'S NOTE

❯ *No specific medical advice for this expression.*

## BREEDS

• **This expression is not limited to specific breeds.**

 ## WHAT YOUR DOG WANTS

Fearful or anxious dogs make quick glances at people or dogs they view as intimidating, and may even do a few cheek puffs to try to calm themselves.

Happy dogs who want your attention make energetic sideways glances your way and may play bow to deliver hard-to-mistake clues that playtime should start—now! They are bubbling with energy and long to play fetch, tug-of-war, or another favorite game with you.

Socialized, confident dogs know that it is rude to stare during dog-to-dog introductions. They glance at other dogs and look away in the initial sniff-and-greet.

## ✓ HOW TO RESPOND

It is totally acceptable to let your dog initiate play at times, but do not let her become pushy or demanding. Maintain your benevolent leadership role by having her get into a "sit" or "stay" postion at the start of play, and let her know with a voice or hand signal when the game is over.

Loosen her leash when she meets another leashed dog and maintain a calm, confident posture to improve the odds of a friendly introduction.

BEHAVIOR TYPES: **Anxious/Stressed** *p.179* • **Attention-seeking** *p.179* • **Fearful** *p.182* • **Happy** *p.182* • **Playful** *p.183* • **Submissive** *p.185*

# 22 Open-mouthed Sniffing

- ○ Your dog's mouth forms an "O" shape while she sniffs.

- ○ After you spend time with a new dog, your dog sniffs your pant leg with an open mouth.

## BREEDS

- American Foxhound
- Basset Hound
- Beagle
- Bloodhound
- Bulldog
- Coonhound
- Dachshund
- Pug
- Siberian Husky

### WHAT YOUR DOG WANTS

With dogs, the nose knows. Your dog can smell more than a thousand times better than you can. One reason is because she has a vomeronasal organ located near the palate, which gives her the enhanced ability to taste a smell, as well as smell it.

Dogs use their noses to track, trail, and air sniff. Scent hounds, such as Bloodhounds and Beagles, are bred to track and scent prey. They open their mouths while sniffing an area to pinpoint the specific scent.

### HOW TO RESPOND

Your dog uses her powerful sense of smell to gather clues and information, in the same way that a human detective would work on a case.

After spending time with a friend's new dog, allow your dog a few minutes to sniff your clothing and gather canine information. Be calm and do not shoo her away. You want her to be exposed to this new dog's scent, so when they do meet it will be a friendly interaction.

### VET'S NOTE

❯ Short-nosed dog breeds, known as brachycephalic breeds, such as Pugs or Bulldogs, are prone to breathing problems. They do not tolerate long exposure to hot temperatures and the open-mouth expression may progress to excessive panting.

BEHAVIOR TYPES: Curious *p.181* • Predatory *p.184*

# 23 Lip Licking

○ Your dog's mouth is not just made for barking, drinking, and eating. It can also mirror her mood.

○ In less than a second, your dog uses her tongue like a windshield wiper to lick off the dab of peanut butter you placed on her nose.

○ Some shy dogs quickly lick their noses during dog-to-dog introductions.

○ Dogs temporarily stymied by a new move in agility training may lick their lips while trying to come up with a solution.

**BREEDS**

● This expression is not limited to specific breeds.

**WHAT YOUR DOG WANTS**

A dog may lick her lips when she feels uneasy or unsure during an introduction. She may also make this expression if she is nervous during her first day of obedience training in a class of unfamiliar dogs. By licking her lips your dog says to her canine classmates, "I want to make sure you know I am okay."

Some anxious dogs may lick their noses repeatedly, glance sideways, and raise their eyes so you can see the white underneath. This is similar to a nervous person who bites their fingernails.

Dogs enrolled in obedience, agility, or other types of formal classes that require mastery of different skills may repeatedly lick their lips while they concentrate.

Lower-ranking dogs or young pups show deference and respect to higher-ranking or mature adult dogs by licking their lips or the muzzle of the superior dog.

Placing peanut butter or processed cheese spread on the tip of your dog's nose will cause her to happily use her tongue to clean the nose and enjoy the tasty treat. Some dogs lick their lips when you pull a roast out of the oven or when they sense you are preparing other food that emits a powerful, beckoning aroma.

 **HOW TO RESPOND**

Before you take your dog to her first day of obedience class, or any other structured dog class, treat her to a run, brisk walk, or vigorous game of fetch. The goal is to channel her energy in a positive way so that she will be a little tired and a lot more relaxed when she enters the class of dogs she does not yet know.

Do not succumb to your dog's begging when you prepare a meal. She will do her best to win some food by staring at you, perhaps whining a little, and even licking her lips. Block the kitchen during meal preparation time with dog gates or keep your dog busy with a toy in another closed-off room.

 **VET'S NOTE**

› *Your dog may persistently lick her lips, also known as tongue flicking, because of mouth pain or an injury to the mouth or nose that warrants medical attention.*
› *Obsessive-compulsive dogs cannot break repetitive behaviors and may lick their lips while they circle or pace up and down.*

# 24 Open, Relaxed Mouth

○ The tongue is draped over the lower teeth, hangs limply from one side of the mouth, or droops straight out.

○ Look for soft eyes that do not stare and ears up or cupped.

## BREEDS

• Border Collie
• Chow Chow
• Finnish Spitz
• German Shepherd
• Golden Retriever
• Great Pyrenees
• Old English Sheepdog
• Pug
• Schipperke
• Siberian Husky

## VET'S NOTE

❯ No specific medical advice for this expression.

## WHAT YOUR DOG WANTS

In the dog world, this is the ultimate grin. Certain breeds sport wider grins than others, especially those with long muzzles, such as German Shepherds and Golden Retrievers.

Confident, happy dogs who feel safe in their environment often display this open-mouthed expression. They perceive no threats or problems, and are usually in relaxed or upbeat moods.

Some dogs open their mouths and pant after a vigorous run or game of fetch to cool down. If your dog is overheated, dip her paws in cool, not cold, water to help her drop her body temperature safely.

## HOW TO RESPOND

Share in your dog's good mood. Give her a belly rub or come up with a jingle that includes your dog's name and happily sing it to her. She will not care if you sing off-key—she loves the positive attention.

Indulge your dog with a play session or her favorite treat, but make sure you do not let her become pushy or bossy.

BEHAVIOR TYPES: Affectionate p.178 • Attention-seeking p.179 • Confident p.180 • Happy p.182

# 25 Mouth Stiffly Closed

○ Your focused dog may be telling you, "Hang on a second, I am checking something out and need to concentrate."

○ Think of this gesture as a dog's silent warning not to take one more step closer. Otherwise, she is prepared to lunge and snap at you.

## BREEDS

• This expression is not limited to specific breeds.

## VET'S NOTE

❯ *No specific medical advice for this expression.*

## WHAT YOUR DOG WANTS

An alert or curious dog closes her mouth, perks up her ears, and widens her eyes. She may stand on all four paws or wiggle slightly, with tail up or moving slowly.

An anxious or fearful dog also closes her mouth, but her ears are back or flattened against her head, her body is tense, and she may emit a low whine or moan. You can see the whites in her eyes.

A dominant or aggressive dog keeps her mouth closed and stands tall. Her body is stiff and tense, and her hackles may be raised. Before striking, she bears her teeth and makes low growls.

## HOW TO RESPOND

Before you make a snap judgment call on your dog's mood, step back and look at her body language from head to tail. It is easy to misinterpret a dog's true emotional state if you judge strictly by a closed mouth.

If two dogs are staring at each other with stiffly closed mouths, widen the distance between them.

BEHAVIOR TYPES: **Aggressive** *p.178* • **Anxious/Stressed** *p.179* • **Curious** *p.181* • **Dominant** *p.181* • **Fearful** *p.182* • **Predatory** *p.184*

# 26 Head Tilting

o An attentive dog often responds to your chatter with non-blinking eyes and the tilting of her head to one side.

o Some dogs master the ability to cock their heads from one side to the other in steady cadence.

o Norwegian Lundehunds can tilt their heads backward along their spine.

o Without a single yap or bark, your dog is telling you that she is, literally, "all ears" and fully focused on you.

## BREEDS

- Australian Shepherd
- Basenji
- Bernese Mountain Dog
- Border Collie
- Cairn Terrier
- Chihuahua
- Collie
- Corgi
- Jack (Parson) Russell Terrier
- Norwegian Lundehunds
- Poodle
- Pug
- Schnauzer

## WHAT YOUR DOG WANTS

Dogs do their best to get the gist of our spoken words by stopping what they are doing, sitting or standing still, erecting their ears, shifting their head to one side, and delivering a relaxed but curious pose.

Pay close attention the next time there are people around. Notice that dogs tend to reserve this head maneuver only for the person who is right in front of them. It is especially evident if that person uses a magic word, such as "treat."

Some dogs also tilt their heads when attempting to tune into a fuzzy sound or strange noise in order to pinpoint its identity and location. They rely heavily on their superior sense of hearing to compensate for their lack of opposable thumbs or extensive vocabulary.

Dog ears come in many shapes, from long and floppy to upright and pointed. Each dog has her own way of capturing and perceiving sound.

Uncontrolled head tilting can be caused by a serious problem that requires vet attention.

## VET'S NOTE

> *Some dogs cannot control the head tilts because of medical issues. Topping the list: ear infections. Your dog's ear canals may contain ear mites, bacteria, or a foreign object, such as a foxtail.*
> *Other less common causes include: toxic reaction to some antibiotics, cancer, encephalitis, head injury, hypothyroidism, and vestibular disease.*

## HOW TO RESPOND

Smart dogs quickly discover that this cute pose can yield them oodles of treats and praise. Harness your dog's benign head-tilting tendencies to make training sessions more fun. Reinforce desired actions, such as head tilting, as part of your dog's repertoire of mastered tricks to delight friends and family.

Conduct regular tutoring sessions, not only to develop new tricks and expand your "people-dog vocabulary," but also to bolster your bond. Your dog will go out of her way to perform her best because you have proven through consistent actions and words that you truly are her best friend.

Equally important, investigate why it is that your dog tilts her head when she is not looking at you. She may be getting an early bead on a sound that warrants your attention, such as a delivery person approaching your walkway. Reward your dog when she sounds the "alarm" so that she is acknowledged for doing her job.

BEHAVIOR TYPES: **Attention-seeking** *p.179* • **Curious** *p.181* • **Obsessive-Compulsive** *p.183*

# 27 Yawning

○ **Look for a wide, open mouth and a breathy exhale or two.**

○ **The eyes are brought to a close as the mouth opens, and the ears are usually back.**

○ **You have just taken your dog on a long, invigorating hike or asked her to roll over for the 15th time.**

## BREEDS

- Australian Shepherd
- Border Collie
- English Springer Spaniel
- Jack (Parson) Russell Terrier
- Poodle

## WHAT YOUR DOG WANTS

Yawning is more apt to indicate stress than fatigue. It is one of the primary go-to calming signals that dogs use. This is the canine equivalent of a person who abruptly switches to a new topic when they suspect a heated—and unwanted—argument is about to erupt. The maneuver is employed to diffuse a potentially explosive situation.

Some dogs, especially intelligent ones who catch on to new tricks quickly, grow tired of long, repetitive training sessions. They may start to yawn and scratch their heads with their back paws as a way to relieve stress, take a break from concentrating too much, and to re-energize.

Just like people, dogs yawn when they are bored and tired of dull routines. They also yawn when they see another dog or person yawn. For unknown reasons, yawning can be contagious.

## VET'S NOTE

> *Yawning has been shown in vet studies to help lower a dog's blood pressure and help her stay calm in a stressful situation. It increases the flow of oxygen to the brain and bolsters the heart rate. Chronically anxious or nervous dogs may need calming medications.*

> *Savvy vets often talk in calm, soothing tones to a dog who is quivering in the exam room. In response, a dog may stand up, shake herself, and let out a big yawn as she rids her body of anxiety.*

## HOW TO RESPOND

Take a break from the intensity and duration of a training session with your dog if you notice that she starts to yawn. She is trying to tell you that she needs a rest. Dogs learn best in mini-sessions. Slowly build, step-by-step, on each success with each training class.

Be clear and concise in communicating with your dog during obedience class, agility training, or other structured activity. If you give conflicting signals or confusing commands, your trying-to-please dog may respond by yawning because she is stressed and anxious. To calm an anxious dog, get her attention, lick your lips, and make a big yawn yourself.

Do not fall into a rut with your dog's daily walks. Break up the routine by taking her to a new place or have one of your dog's canine friends and her owner join you for a walk.

BEHAVIOR TYPES: Anxious/Stressed p.179 • Bored p.180 • Fearful p.182 • Submissive p.185

# 28 Sneezing

○ Your dog is having the best time playing with you.

○ Ouch! Your dog has a foxtail stuck up her nose and she cannot get it out.

○ Look for a wide, open mouth and a breathy exhale or two.

○ The eyes are brought to a close as the mouth opens and the ears are usually back.

### BREEDS

- English Bulldog
- French Bulldog
- Pekingese
- Pug
- Rough Collie

## ? WHAT YOUR DOG WANTS

The sneeze is a handy safety valve for a dog. When a curious dog gets a bit too curious and sniffs a flower or a patch of ground cover, she may accidentally inhale a bee or a twig. She sneezes to expel it from her nostrils.

Sneezing can be an early sign of respiratory infection, which inflames the nasal membranes. A young pup's immune system is still fortifying, so this puts her at greater risk of contracting upper respiratory-tract infections than an adult dog who is up-to-date with all her vaccinations.

For reasons that today remain unexplained, smaller dogs tend to emit quick, short sneezes and paw during gleeful play sessions with other dogs and their favorite people. There is nothing medically wrong—these dogs are just excited. It is similar to a person who leaps up and down with joy at discovering they hold the winning lottery ticket.

## ✓ HOW TO RESPOND

Pay attention to when your dog started to sneeze. Was it right after you returned from a walk in the woods? If so, she may have sniffed too hard and inhaled a burr or other object.

Carefully inspect your dog from snout to tail for foreign objects, especially in her nose and between her toes. Healthy dogs have wet or dry noses but ailing dogs may sneeze, have nasal discharge, or cracked and extremely dry noses.

If her sneezing episodes only occur during spring or early summer, your dog may have a seasonal allergy to pollen or grass.

## VET'S NOTE

> Persistent sneezing may be caused by an allergic reaction to an ingredient in dog food, such as corn or wheat, or to something in the environment, such as grass, pollen, mold, cigarette smoke, or perfume. A vet may run allergy tests to pinpoint the cause.

> Upper respiratory-tract infections caused by bacteria or a virus, such as bordetella, parainfluenza virus, and streptococci, may make dogs sneeze.

> Seek immediate vet care if you see blood in your dog's nasal discharge. This could indicate a tumor or tooth abscess. Also see your vet if sneezing occurs more than four or five times a day, or continues for a few days.

BEHAVIOR TYPES: **Attention-seeking** p.179 • **Happy** p.182 • **Playful** p.183

# 29 Air Snapping with Mouth

- Your dog snaps and bites the air as he tries desperately to catch imaginary flies buzzing by his head.

- During this repetitive behavior, he may lick his front leg excessively.

- Your dog will make little to no vocalizations.

- The cheeks may be puffed with air while your dog makes quick glances to one side.

**WHAT YOUR DOG WANTS**

You do not detect a single bug, but your dog suddenly freezes, lifts his head, and begins snapping his mouth as if he is biting airborne pests. When done to the extreme, this condition is referred to as fly biting.

Air snapping can be coupled with other obsessive-compulsive actions, such as when dogs chase their tails or act as if their paws are irritated. It can progress to being constant during waking hours.

However, some happy, confident dogs snap the air like a crocodile and make quick sideways glances in an effort to tempt their favorite people to engage in play. This is a friendly, attention-seeking behavior.

 **HOW TO RESPOND**

To maintain your higher status, it is vital to determine whether you want to respond to your dog's play invitation at this moment. Be careful not to always drop what you are doing and give in to his air snapping—he will become pushy and demanding.

Do not dismiss air snapping as quirky or harmless if your dog seems to be on a constant hunt for imaginary flies. Also, do not allow your dog's air-snapping episodes to escalate and grow longer. You need to work with a vet, most likely a specialist in internal medicine or neurology, to find the root cause of this behavior and come up with a treatment plan.

**BREEDS**

- Beagle
- Belgian Tervuren
- Cavalier King Charles Spaniel
- German Shepherd
- Golden Retriever
- Keeshond
- Poodle
- Shetland Sheepdog
- Siberian Husky
- Vizsla

**VET'S NOTE**

› *Vet neurologists suspect compulsive, uncontrollable air snapping may be linked to a type of complex partial epileptic seizure. This is a brain disorder that can cause a dog to snap at the air repeatedly. Certain breeds are at greater risk of inheriting epilepsy. Experts theorize that air-snapping dogs may experience hallucinations, but the evidence remains inconclusive.*

› *Dogs with an eye condition known as vitreous floater, when the eye is filled with fluid and a small piece of debris, see black spots in front of their eyes and think that they are flies. A special eye scope is used to determine the presence of any debris in the eye.*

BEHAVIOR TYPES: **Attention-seeking** *p.179* • **Happy** *p.182* • **Obsessive-Compulsive** *p.183* • **Playful** *p.183*

# 30 High-pitched Barking

○ Your hungry young pup lets out a series of ear-splitting cries.

○ Sharp, short barks are delivered to a favorite person or playmate.

○ A squirrel races by and your dog cannot find the mute button.

## BREEDS

• Beagle
• Chihuahua
• Collie
• Shetland Sheepdog
• Yorkshire Terrier

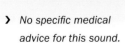

## VET'S NOTE

❯ No specific medical advice for this sound.

### ? WHAT YOUR DOG WANTS

Dogs who feel distressed when left alone sound their displeasure by making high-pitched, drawn-out vocals with pauses in between. The barks get higher in pitch and longer in duration as the dog becomes more upset.

Highly social dogs, who are used to being around other dogs or their favorite people, make this sound in desperation, to try to relieve anxiety when they are left alone in a hotel room or other strange new place. Some dogs just love to greet familiar people and canine friends by unleashing two or three high-pitched, short barks as a sign of affection.

If a dog is caught off guard or startled, he may make a few sharp, short, high-pitched barks as if to convey, "Hey, what is this?"

### ✓ HOW TO RESPOND

The bark, no matter its form, is a way for dogs to communicate their feelings about everything and anything in their world. Investigate to see what your dog is barking at before you react.

Coddling an anxious, high-pitched barking pup only increases his anxiety issues. Instead, speak to him in a calm, confident tone to minimize his stress.

BEHAVIOR TYPES: Anxious/Stressed p.179 • Attention-seeking p.179 • Happy p.182 • Playful p.183

# 31 Rapid Barking

- Quick "wooo-wooo" barks are the canine equivalent of sounding the alarm.

- Your dog's barking becomes faster in tempo and higher in pitch when he cannot retrieve his favorite ball.

- The barks may grow more urgent when your dog is being walked on a leash and he spots a stray cat in his path.

### BREEDS

- Chihuahua
- Dalmatian
- Miniature Schnauzer
- West Highland White Terrier
- Yorkshire Terrier

### VET'S NOTE

> No specific medical advice for this sound.

 ## WHAT YOUR DOG WANTS

Some dogs have a natural distrust of strangers, including people and dogs, and bark quickly to signal their approach to higher-ranking members of the household.

Rapid barking is often triggered when someone rings your doorbell, startling your dog while he naps in the other room.

This form of barking evolves as the dog reaches maturity and is a full-fledged member of the household with a job to do: defend the turf by sounding the alarm.

 ## HOW TO RESPOND

Train your dog to heed your cues when he hears the doorbell. He should learn to move away from the door and wait on a rug or the stair landing, so you can open the door without his interference.

Acknowledge his detection by saying to him calmly, "Okay, I've got it. Go to your spot."

Yelling at your dog to stop barking will backfire and cause him to bark more because he will think that you are joining him in the barking chorus.

BEHAVIOR TYPES: **Anxious/Stressed** *p.179* • **Attention-seeking** *p.179* • **Curious** *p.181* • **Dominant** *p.181*

# 32 Repetitive Barking

o   It feels like a broken record, playing the same bark in the same pitch and the same tempo over and over and over again.

o   Scent hounds bark, bark, and bark to alert owners to their location during a formal chase of prey or on seeing a squirrel at the dog park.

o   A dog left alone in the backyard all day makes a continuous, monotone bark, much to the displeasure of neighbors.

## BREEDS

- Australian Kelpie
- Australian Shepherd
- Border Collie
- Cairn Terrier
- Cocker Spaniel
- Poodle
- Shetland Sheepdog

## WHAT YOUR DOG WANTS

The most common reason that dogs bark repetitively is simple: they are bored and lack the mental or physical stimulation to keep them from behaving like marathon talkers. These dogs have a bad case of the canine "blahs."

Nonstop barking is also a clear sign that in the dog's view, his needs are not being met. Since your dog cannot speak English—or any other human language—he is doing his best to communicate that all is not right in his world.

Herding dogs, such as Border Collies and Australian Shepherds, make urgent, repetitive barks when they herd sheep and cattle, to keep the animals together.

Dogs who are confined to their crates for too long may develop into nuisance barkers out of sheer frustration. Restrict the time that your dog spends in his crate to a maximum of five or six hours a day.

 ## VET'S NOTE

> Frustration-induced barking can lead to destructive behavior, such as pawing doors or chewing furniture legs. A dog's paws and mouth can become bloodied by repetitive scratching and chewing and may need a vet's attention.

 ## HOW TO RESPOND

One word: exercise! Your dog is crying out for the opportunity to do something, to do anything, that works his brain and provides him with exercise. Instead of leaving him home alone every day while you are at work, treat your dog and send him along to a dog daycare center a couple of days a week.

Identify the source of your dog's excessive barking. Look for the "why." Your dog may not like being kept in a crate for long durations. Or he may have discovered repetitive barking gets your attention.

If you live near a four-legged neighborhood noisemaker, then introduce yourself to the offender's owners and inform them that you want to work together to find a solution and restore quiet in the neighborhood. You can suggest that they give their dog long-lasting treats, such as a hollow hard-rubber toy stuffed with cheese, kibble, or peanut butter. Also, inform them about special dog collars that are designed to control excessive barking by emitting citronella spray.

# 33 Growling

- ○ When a dog is ready to attack, he barks first and bares his teeth before he progresses to making low, throaty "grrrr" sounds.

- ○ This is often the last verbal warning before a dog bites.

- ○ A dog engaged in a tug-of-war game may make mock growls during play.

**VET'S NOTE**

> *Injured dogs may growl when examined because they are in pain. Fortunately, great strides have been made in effective pain-management medications for dogs. However, you may still need to put a safety muzzle on your injured dog while transporting him to the clinic, to prevent him from biting you because of the pain.*

## WHAT YOUR DOG WANTS

Growls come in different pitches and durations and are made by dogs of all sizes, breeds, and ages.

A nervous dog who is frightened, but ready to defend himself if you come any closer, delivers a high-pitched growl-bark.

A dominant, confident, or aggressive dog who is ordering—not asking—you to back off or else he will bite, emits a low-pitched, deep growl that seems to come from the chest. It grows in intensity just before the dog attacks.

Resource-guarding dogs growl to maintain control of their prized possessions. They have learned that by growling they get to make the rules.

Older dogs growl in order to get playful pups to change direction and leave them alone.

Not all growls are fierce. Confident, well-socialized dogs emit low growls during active play. They display play bows, soft eyes, and relaxed bodies, and are inviting you to play like a dog—this is the ultimate canine compliment.

Certain dogs, such as German Shepherds, undergo extensive training to become police dogs. They follow growl cues from their handlers when dealing with criminal suspects.

### BREEDS

- This sound is not limited to specific breeds.

## HOW TO RESPOND

Never approach a strange dog quickly and face-to-face, especially when he is growling. This is threatening in the dog world. Instead, stand still and let the dog approach and sniff you, if he desires. Otherwise, leave him alone for your safety.

Factor in the context of a growl and exercise caution. Dogs physically punished for growling learn to bite without warning. This is dangerous. Work with a professional dog trainer to address your dog's anger issues.

To retrain resource-guarding dogs, use behavior-modification techniques. Incorporate the "nothing in life is free" training concept with your bossy dog. Bring out a specific toy, set the start and stop time, and have your dog get in a "sit" or "stay" position in order to earn the right to play. The goal of this exercise is to shift his view of you from his servant to someone who outranks him as the benevolent keeper of all good things.

BEHAVIOR TYPES: Aggressive p.178 • Dominant p.181 • Fearful p.182 • Playful p.183 • Predatory p.184

# 34 Howling

○ Anyone interested in a little K9 Karaoke? Welcome to "mutt mike night."

○ Dogs do not need cell phones to communicate over a great distance— howls are free and effective ways to locate another pack member.

○ Scent hounds sing out when they locate prey during a hunt.

○ Certain Nordic breeds do not need a full moon to deliver soul-filled songs.

## BREEDS

• Alaskan Malamute
• Basset Hound
• Beagle
• Foxhound
• Siberian Husky

## WHAT YOUR DOG WANTS

As descendants of wolves and coyotes, two species well known for their vocals, it is not surprising that howling is as natural to most dogs as barking. Howling is a sound made by members of the pack to communicate their locations. A lost dog may howl to alert others looking for him.

The origins of howling are not known, but centuries ago, folklore suggested that dogs howl when evil spirits are around or when the Grim Reaper has arrived and someone is about to die.

Some dogs howl repeatedly in regular intervals if they are suffering from extreme pain or have been spooked by something strange in their surroundings.

Dogs have a far superior sense of hearing than we do. The sound of a siren can be at such an irritatingly high pitch that it can cause some dogs to howl their displeasure. And, do not be offended, but some dogs howl at people who sing off-key—or join them in a song.

Dogs are capable of learning dozens of words and some breeds, particularly the Siberian Husky, delight in making happy howling sounds to converse with you.

Other dogs howl excessively when they grieve for a person or canine they adored.

 ## HOW TO RESPOND

If your dog howls every time he hears a siren—even from the television set—work with a professional dog trainer to use desensitization and counter-conditioning techniques to help your dog find the mute button and reduce his stress.

Instead of yelling at your dog to stop howling, focus on rewarding him for being quiet. Randomly dole out healthy treats when he is not making any noise and make him wait five to ten seconds in silence before you give him his meal or favorite toy. The lesson you are teaching him is that howling reaps nothing, but being quiet provides plenty of rewards.

You can also train your dog to speak when given a specific cue, to channel his need to howl more appropriately.

 ## VET'S NOTE

> *Dogs who suffer from severe separation anxiety howl excessively. Other signs of distress include pacing, house soiling, or destructive chewing. A vet may need to prescribe these dogs antianxiety medications.*

# 35 Panting

○ **Dog panting is the human equivalent of sweaty palms caused by worry.**

○ **Your dog set a personal best in retrieving and needs to catch his breath.**

○ **An exhausted dog opens his mouth, rolls out his tongue, and breathes heavily and quickly.**

## VET'S NOTE

❯ *Brachycephalic breeds—dogs with short noses or pushed-in faces—have more breathing difficulties than dogs with long muzzles. This puts them at greater risk of respiratory problems. Because of their facial structures, it is harder for them to cool down and hot temperatures can cause heat stress.*

❯ *Panting may be coupled with other symptoms, such as vomiting, diarrhea, or a swollen abdomen that warrant immediate vet attention.*

❯ *A dog with a heart or lung condition will get out of breath easily and pant excessively.*

## ? WHAT YOUR DOG WANTS

Some dogs pant when they are too hot, scared, or physically exhausted. All of these reasons can raise your dog's body temperature.

Normal body temperature for a healthy dog is between 100 and 102.5° Fahrenheit (38 and 39°C). A couple degrees above this can cause a dog to pant vigorously as he tries desperately to cool down his body. Dogs do not sweat through skin pores like people do, but rather through the pads of their feet. Overheated dogs leave wet paw marks on the floor caused by sweating.

Some dogs pant because they feel scared, anxious, or tense—emotions that can raise body temperatures and trigger panting episodes.

Dogs pant when they have exercised too much. Some dogs who are obsessed with playing fetch will keep running until they eventually drop over from sheer exhaustion.

## BREEDS

- American Bulldog
- Boston Terrier
- Boxer
- Cavalier King Charles Spaniel
- English Bulldog
- Irish Setter
- Pekingese
- Pug
- Shih Tzu

## ✓ HOW TO RESPOND

If your dog is panting because he is overheated, get him into a ventilated area and cool him down slowly by placing his paws in cool water or wrapping his body in a cool, wet towel. The paws are where dogs sweat and cooling them helps to restore the body's normal core temperature. Do not place your dog in ice-cold water—this extreme change in temperature can shock the dog's body.

Never put your dog in a crate in the corner of a room with towels on top. You will block any ventilation and he may start panting because he is overheated. And certainly never leave your dog inside a closed car on a warm day. The temperature inside a vehicle can resemble that of an oven.

Do not over-exercise your dog, especially on a hot day, by taking him for an overly long run. Build up his endurance gradually and schedule your runs together when temperatures are cool.

Enroll in a pet first-aid class and learn how to recognize normal behavior and early danger signs of panting, so that you can quickly spot any unsafe changes.

BEHAVIOR TYPES: Anxious/Stressed p.179 • Fearful p.182 • Obsessive-Compulsive p.183 • Playful p.183

# 36 Whining

- The mouth is usually closed when a dog produces this nasal, high-pitched sound.

- Your dog does not want to urinate in the house, but desperately needs someone to let him out in the backyard to relieve himself—right now!

- Your dog has seen his favorite canine pal at the dog park and is pleading with you to hurry up and take off his leash so he can dash over.

- A dog at the local humane shelter rushes to the front of his cage and moans in the hope that you will adopt him.

- A young pup may whine if scared when left alone for a few hours.

## WHAT YOUR DOG WANTS

There are self-serving whines and there are genuine "I-need-help" whines. The "want" whines are often produced by lap dogs and toy breeds who have discovered that making faux pleas garners them plenty of attention and pampering from their owners. These dogs emit a charming whine to win a piece of steak from your plate or whine longingly at you from the back door when they want to come inside.

Like children, and some adults, dogs can throw tantrums and whine when they do not get their way or you dare to take away a favorite toy.

However, serious whining occurs when a dog is in pain or desperately needs help. A dog left outside by accident whines and paws at the front door to come in.

Young pups whine when first separated because they feel alone and scared. In an unknown environment, they wonder where their mom and littermates are.

 ## BREEDS

- Bichon Frise
- Cavalier King Charles Spaniel
- English Toy Spaniel
- Japanese Chin
- Maltese
- Miniature Poodle
- Pomeranian
- Shih Tzu
- Toy Poodle
- Yorkshire Terrier

 ## HOW TO RESPOND

Be strong and do not give in to demanding whines. If you cater to his every whim, your dog will soon have you wrapped around his paw. Instead, have him perform a trick for a treat. He must "sit" first before you open the door to the backyard. Or he must hold a "stay" before you give him a healthy treat. Praise him calmly so he does not become overly excited.

Some dogs whine when being crate trained. Make the crate an inviting canine condo by lining the floor with a thick plush pad or blanket. Provide a safe chew toy and water. Put the crate in a place your dog feels safe, not near a front window where he will feel defenseless if a person approaches your front walk.

 ## VET'S NOTE

> If you cannot figure out why your dog is suddenly whining, have him checked by a vet because he may have an underlying medical condition.
> Some dogs whine after surgery and may benefit from pain-relief medication.

BEHAVIOR TYPES: Anxious/Stressed p.179 • Attention-seeking p.179 • Fearful p.182 • Playful p.183 • Sad p.184

# 37 Yapping

- This quick, urgent bark means your dog wants answers—now.

- The yapping sound tops the list of nuisance barking.

- Yap champions are usually not afraid or in pain—they are filled with impatience.

- You may find yourself wishing for earplugs around these dogs.

## BREEDS

- Airedale
- Boston Terrier
- Chihuahua
- French Bulldog
- Irish Setter
- Miniature Pinscher
- Norwegian Elkhound
- Pekingese
- Schnauzer
- Shetland Sheepdog

## WHAT YOUR DOG WANTS

Dogs bark in a variety of tones and cadences to express a wide spectrum of feelings, which can include anxiety, excitement, boredom, play, territorial protection, and aggression. Most often, a dog yaps because he feels extremely territorial. In the dog world, a yapping bark clearly says to the intruder, "Hey! This is MY neighborhood. Who gave YOU permission to walk here?"

Certain dogs are just born yappers. Topping the list for the gift of gab are dogs who are bred to sound alerts, such as terriers and hunting dogs. These breeds are genetically wired to communicate—and sometimes they do so a little loudly.

Occasionally, bored dogs yap just to break up the monotony of their dull day.

## VET'S NOTE

> *No specific medical advice for this sound.*

## HOW TO RESPOND

You can train a dog not to bark, or at least to tone it down, but do not expect to accomplish this in one training session. Be patient. Start by identifying and removing the triggers that seem to get your dog all jazzed up. For example, if your dog races up to the front window to "yap-yap-yap" at leashed dogs as they walk by on the sidewalk, block off his access to this window or close the blinds.

If your dog has superior hearing that leads to frenzied reactions in response to sounds outside, muffle the sounds that trigger his yapping by turning on the radio or playing some background music.

Consult a professional dog trainer about selecting an anti-bark collar that emits a puff of citronella spray, or just plain air, when a dog starts yapping. Dogs do not like this citrus smell and especially do not like the sound. They find it annoying and learn quickly that they can prevent the spray and sound from occurring by not barking.

Use a hand signal, such as a stop sign, in front of your dog's face to get him to quieten down. Do not say a word. Reward him when he is quiet for a few seconds at first, then gradually increase the time he must be silent before you hand over a treat. You are reconditioning him to understand that great rewards will come his way when he finds his mute button and is not yapping.

BEHAVIOR TYPES: **Attention-seeking** *p.179* • **Bored** *p.180*

# 38 Yelping

○ Your puppy lets out a single, quick, high-pitched bark to cry "ouch!" to a sibling who is playing too rough.

○ Your dog makes a soft, high-pitched sound after cutting his paw on broken glass.

○ Your senior dog cries out when he moves his arthritic-riddled body too quickly.

**BREEDS**

• This sound is not limited to specific breeds.

**WHAT YOUR DOG WANTS**

When it comes to announcing pain, your dog is no actor; he will never pretend or bluff. Even with their tough paw pads and coats, dogs are not invincible to pain caused by injury or illness. Your dog will whimper or yelp when he is in pain—be it physical or emotional.

Your dog may have caught his tail in the closing door or pulled muscles after soaring to catch a flying disc and landing on the ground the wrong way. Or he may have been on the losing end of a dogfight and is now seriously injured with deep bite wounds.

When a dog sounds a single yelp, it is the equivalent of the human "ouch!" But a series of yelps is a dog's way of declaring fear and his desperate desire to leave a scary scene or to surrender.

Some dogs yelp when they are startled. A common example of this is when your dog leaps into the air and lets out a yelp in response to the sound of a muffler backfiring from a car parked in a driveway, which your dog happened to be striding past while on his walk.

Fast-growing pups need to learn dog etiquette, especially bite inhibition. In this scenario, the yelp is used to tell another pup that his needle-sharp teeth are biting too deeply during play wrestling.

 **HOW TO RESPOND**

Do not dismiss the yelp as your dog's way to seek attention. If you hear your dog yelp, then he urgently needs your help. He is not giving off harmless yapping.

Dogs with arthritis need your help to minimize the pain in their joints. Consider taking your dog to a dog water-therapy class or learn how to perform therapeutic massages to ease his aches and improve his circulation and blood flow.

For joint comfort, improved flexibility, and greater mobility, add a canine joint supplement to your dog's diet that contains glucosamine-chondroitin, or shark cartilage. Work with a pet professional to get the right dosage for your dog.

 **VET'S NOTE**

> *Dogs who cry out when touched may have a serious bruise, broken bone, or internal injury that needs to be examined and treated by a vet. X-rays may be needed to pinpoint the source of the pain.*
> *Consider feeding your dog foods rich in omega-6 fatty acids to ease achy joints. Work with your vet to select a commercial brand that best meets your dog's breed, age, activity level, and medical condition.*

# 39 Chewing or Licking Paws

- ○ The sound of your dog licking her paws all night long is driving you crazy.

- ○ Your Chow Chow sits on the patio gnawing at her feet all day.

- ○ Your white Poodle has orange feet and missing hair from constant licking.

- ○ Your dog's paw is inflamed from her relentless chewing.

## BREEDS

- Borzoi
- Bull Terrier
- Chow Chow
- English Bulldog
- Golden Retriever
- Great Dane
- Great Pyrenees
- Poodle

## WHAT YOUR DOG WANTS

Your dog may want to relieve itchiness in her paws, which has been caused by an allergy or a nail-bed infection. She may also have developed an obsessive-compulsive behavior that results in paw licking, or she may be suffering from nerve damage that has been caused by trauma. In the case of nerve damage, your dog may chew on her paw because she is experiencing an uncomfortable feeling in her skin and is trying to relieve the sensation.

Dogs also chew and lick their paws because these actions produce endorphins, which are chemicals that signal pleasure in the brain.

However, chewing and licking the paws can become a vicious cycle. A dog may start chewing or licking because her paw feels itchy or uncomfortable, which makes the skin irritated. This irritation, in turn, encourages the dog to chew or lick even more for relief, which causes further irritation, and so on.

## VET'S NOTE

> *If you notice that your dog persistently gnaws her paws, look for evidence of burrs, stickers, or foxtails.*
> *Dogs who chew or lick their paws are susceptible to developing lick granulomas, which are areas on the paw where the skin becomes red and inflamed. The granuloma can become infected and may need a vet's attention.*

## HOW TO RESPOND

Before you can help your dog with her problem, you need to find out what is going on. If she chews and licks her paws because they feel itchy, she probably has an allergy. Take her to the vet for allergy testing. She may be allergic to her diet, or pollen could be the culprit. If she has an infection in her nails, a vet can treat this condition and relieve the itch.

Sometimes a dog initially licks and chews at her paws because of itching, but goes on to continue this action after the initial problem is resolved. If this happens, she suffers from a behavioral issue that can be exacerbated by boredom and stress. Your dog needs help from a professional. A vet may prescribe medication to help your dog deal with her stress and break her chewing and licking habit. Or an animal behaviorist may be able to create a solution for your dog that will help reduce her urge to lick and chew.

BEHAVIOR TYPES: **Anxious/Stressed** *p.179* • **Bored** *p.180* • **Obsessive-Compulsive** *p.183*

# 40 Chewing Objects

○ Your family's shoes are riddled with puncture holes.

○ Shreds of your sofa pillows litter the living-room floor.

○ The coffee table is missing a leg and tilts like a capsized ship. In the midst of this mayhem is your tail-thumping dog, eager to greet you.

○ You were only gone an hour. How, why, did your dog turn into a chewing machine?

## BREEDS

- American Staffordshire Terrier
- Beagle
- Border Collie
- Boxer
- Chesapeake Bay Retriever
- Chihuahua
- Golden Retriever
- Jack (Parson) Russell Terrier
- Labrador Retriever
- Portuguese Water Dog
- Pug
- Schnauzer
- Siberian Husky
- Staffordshire Bull Terrier

## WHAT YOUR DOG WANTS

Natural explorers, dogs investigate their surroundings by heeding the canine motto: sniff, taste, and chew. Teething pups need things to chew to offset sore gums.

Behavior issues also unleash destructive chewing habits. Dogs left home alone for long hours counter boredom, restlessness, and separation anxiety by sinking their teeth into the baseboard or turning toilet paper rolls into confetti. Some dogs are so emotionally attached to their owners that they augment their absence by chewing on inappropriate objects as a way to self-medicate and reclaim a sense of calm. Other chewers demand attention by selecting something bearing your scent and ravaging it in front of you.

Dogs with oodles of energy and no positive outlet will chew on anything and everything.

Your dog's health status can also trigger harmful chewing of her own body. Dogs trying to fend off fleas or food allergies chew their fur, feet, and skin to find relief from intense itching.

 ## VET'S NOTE

> *Dogs with severe separation anxiety or thunderstorm phobia may chew to escape the scene and require calming medication from a vet.*
> *A dog who chews off fur and nibbles through her skin may suffer from a hotspot or fleabites. Dogs with hypothyroidism may chew on their bodies.*

 ## HOW TO RESPOND

Before you rename your dog "Jaws," zero in on the diverse reasons dogs chew. All dogs, big and small, young and old, need and deserve constructive physical and mental stimulation on a regular basis. Just like us, they benefit from physical workouts and brain-fortifying challenges. Remember, a well-exercised dog is a happy dog.

Keep your dog engaged by taking the ho-hum out of daily walks. Vary the route, duration, and tempo. Add to the fun by working on new tricks that yield tasty treats when mastered. Both of you will return home refreshed and better bonded.

Before you bring home your puppy or adult dog, dog-proof each room to put away chew temptations, such as shoes or pillows, at least until the chew phase has passed. Never give your pup an old slipper to chew—you are teaching her that all shoes are fair game. Instead, provide appropriate chew objects, such as rubber toys or synthetic hollow bones you can stuff with food.

BEHAVIOR TYPES: **Anxious/Stressed** *p.179* • **Attention-seeking** *p.179* • **Bored** *p.180* • **Curious** *p.181* • **Fearful** *p.182*

# 41 Gutting Stuffed Toys

○ "Boredom be gone!" declares your home-alone dog as she prepares to feast on her monkey-shaped dog toy.

○ Ten minutes after you gave your terrier mix a brand-new plush toy, your living-room carpet is littered with white, billowy fabric and your dog is smiling in triumph.

○ Sorry folks, but dogs do not distinguish between children's toys and dog toys, which explains why your toddler's stuffed plump bear is now deflated.

## BREEDS

- Beagle
- Cairn Terrier
- Cocker Spaniel
- Coonhound
- English Springer Spaniel
- Foxhound
- Siberian Husky

## WHAT YOUR DOG WANTS

Despite the fact that dogs have been domesticated for thousands of years, they have never lost their hunting instinct. Though we humans provide them with plenty of good food and healthy treats, dogs need, and want, to hone their hunting skills. Lacking access to real prey, dogs stalk and "kill" pretend prey—plush toys. Terrier, sporting, and hunting breeds lead the pack when it comes to gutting stuffed toys.

Some dogs take great delight in using their teeth to surgically open the toy and toss out the stuffing to retrieve the squeaker. This is the canine equivalent to a person finding the prize in a box of candy.

Dogs who are extremely bored or anxious need something to do, and chewing is a favorite way for these dogs to pass the time or sooth frayed nerves. Gutting a toy gives dogs a sense of accomplishment. It also serves as an outlet for excess energy.

## VET'S NOTE

> In a dog's hasty determination to gut a toy, she may swallow the squeaker or stuffing, which can cause stomach or small intestinal blockages, and require surgery. Take your dog to a vet if she seems to have abdominal pain, drools, lacks an appetite, acts lethargic, or is vomiting.

## HOW TO RESPOND

Supervise your dog while she plays hunter on a plush toy and clean up any of the spilled contents immediately, so that she cannot accidentally swallow it and choke.

To increase the challenge of gutting a stuffed toy, wrap the toy in an old T-shirt and tie the ends off, place it inside a box or hide it somewhere else, then encourage your dog to hunt and sniff it out. All of these strategies will provide both the mental and physical stimulation your dog craves.

Replacing plush toys can be expensive. Introduce your dog to more durable toys, such as hollow, hard rubber ones. You can fill these toys with pieces of kibble or smear them with peanut butter, cream cheese, plain yogurt, or any of your dog's other favorite foods.

Match the size of the toy with the size of your dog. Avoid giving her small toys that can be easily swallowed.

BEHAVIOR TYPES: **Anxious/Stressed** *p.179* • **Attention-seeking** *p.179* • **Bored** *p.180* • **Playful** *p.183* • **Predatory** *p.184*

# 42 Scooting

**BREEDS**

- This action is not limited to specific breeds.

o Ugh, what timing. Your dog drags her bottom across your newly cleaned carpet, creating a dark brown potty path in the living room, right before dinner guests arrive.

o You experience both disgust and amazement when your dog demonstrates her extreme coordination by sliding along on her bottom, powered only by her front paws.

o Your dog may convey, "Who needs toilet paper when this plush carpet is so much nicer on my bottom?"

## WHAT YOUR DOG WANTS

Time for a little canine rear-end anatomy lesson. Dogs have an anal sac on either side of their anus. The sacs are located in the four o'clock and eight o'clock positions around the anus. These round pouches release a foul-smelling liquid that, while disgusting to your nose, serves as your dog's identification card—a means of leaving her details for other sniffing dogs.

Dogs drag their bottoms across grass or carpet to relieve both the pain and the itch that is associated with swollen anal glands.

Your dog's anal gland issues may be attributed to an inferior diet or eating inappropriate foods.

Size does matter. Scooting seems to strike more often in small dogs than in large dogs.

## VET'S NOTE

> The two main culprits that cause your dog to perform this disgusting and stinky act are infected anal sacs and the presence of parasites, in particular tapeworms.
> A vet will manually express your dog's infected anal sac and may also prescribe an antibiotic. If your dog has tapeworms or other parasites, deworming tablets will be prescribed.
> Untreated, the sacs can burst and require surgical repair.

## HOW TO RESPOND

Keep tabs on your dog's bathroom habits and check her rear after she makes a "deposit" in the grass. If you spot fecal matter clinging to the hair around the anus, remove it and inspect the anal glands.

Check your dog's stool for signs of tapeworms. These parasites look like grains of uncooked rice.

Ask a professional dog groomer to express your dog's anal glands regularly, to prevent them from becoming impacted and infected. Have hair around your dog's anal glands cropped to lessen the chance of fecal matter getting caught in her fur.

Show how much you truly love your dog by having your groomer or vet teach you how to express your dog's anal glands. Do this when you bath your dog. Wear latex gloves and squeeze out the yellowish-tan liquid on a clean paper towel.

If your dog produces stools that are too hard or too soft, consult your vet about selecting a diet that will help your dog to form healthy stools.

BEHAVIOR TYPES: Anxious/Stressed p.179 • Sexual p.185

# 43 Roaming

○ No matter what you do, you cannot keep your "Houdini dog" inside the fenced backyard.

○ Someone left the back gate open and your Siberian Husky is nowhere to be found.

○ You keep getting calls from neighbors and the animal shelter because your dog is found wandering the streets.

## BREEDS

- Airedale
- Beagle
- Dogue de Bordeaux
- Flat-coated Retriever
- Labrador Retriever
- Siberian Husky

## WHAT YOUR DOG WANTS

Dogs who roam are seeking something. If your dog is not neutered or spayed, he or she is looking for a mate and roaming is a great way to hook up with another dog. Sexual hormones are strong motivators, and prompt dogs to find just about any way possible to get out of confinement, with the goal of breeding. Males run around the neighborhood searching for the scent of a female dog in heat, while females in heat roam to put themselves out there, where a meandering male may find them.

Unaltered dogs usually lose the urge to roam once they are spayed or neutered. A few months after dogs have this surgery, their sexual hormones subside and they become homebodies, content to hang around the house and stay close to their human companions.

Bored dogs wander around the neighborhood looking for something to do or in the hope of finding a little companionship. Other dogs roam because they are anxious from being left alone.

 ## VET'S NOTE

> *Roaming is one of the most dangerous behaviors a dog can exhibit. Dogs who roam are more likely to get hit by cars or to be injured in a dogfight.*
> *Spaying and neutering are safe surgeries that not only reduce a dog's desire to roam, but also decrease the likelihood of the dog developing certain types of cancers.*

 ## HOW TO RESPOND

To keep a dog from roaming, give her more attention and exercise. Do not leave her outside for long periods of time. Make her part of the family so that she bonds closely to you and loses her desire to roam. Take her for walks, play ball with her, and let her stay inside as much as possible, so she can be close to the family.

Dogs who are bored, anxious, or lonely seek excitement and company. If you leave your dog alone in the backyard for hours on end, she is likely to go stir-crazy and feel desperate for some stimulation. There may be no better way for her to get that stimulation than by taking a jaunt around the neighborhood to see what is going on. To your dog, getting loose means being able to sniff fire hydrants, visit with other dogs, and maybe even find a friendly human along the way.

BEHAVIOR TYPES: Anxious/Stressed *p.179* • Attention-seeking *p.179* • Bored *p.180* • Curious *p.181*

# 44 Chasing Animals

○ When on a walk, your dog just about rips your arm out of the socket if she sees a squirrel, duck, or other bird.

○ Your poor cat cannot walk through the house without your dog bolting after her.

○ Your neighbor will not speak to you anymore because your dog keeps harassing his animals.

## BREEDS

- American Eskimo Dog
- American Foxhound
- Border Collie
- Cardigan Welsh Corgi
- Doberman Pinscher
- Irish Water Spaniel
- Jack (Parson) Russell Terrier
- Saluki

**WHAT YOUR DOG WANTS**

Dogs who run after other animals think they have discovered the world's most enjoyable sport. The problem is that, in many cases, it is not so much fun for the other animals, or humans involved.

Some dogs harass another animal to get it in their jaws and chomp on the poor creature. To these dogs, it is all about the hunt, capture, and kill. Other dogs delight in the chase. For these dogs, chasing animals is more of a friendly sport and a way for them to test their running skills.

Certain dogs, particularly herding breeds such as Border Collies and corgis, are genetically wired to chase targeted animals, and once they have caught up to them, to herd the animals in a specific direction. For these dogs, chasing animals is part of their innate nature.

**VET'S NOTE**

> *If your dog is fast enough to make contact with an animal she is chasing, she may end up getting hurt. Cats will scratch and bite a dog who catches them and a horse can land a deadly blow to a dog who is close on its heels.*

 **HOW TO RESPOND**

A dog who enjoys the pursuit of other animals to a dangerous degree, where she ignores your command to "stay," needs her urge to chase redirected. Spend time encouraging her to chase a ball instead of another animal and let her know that it is not okay to harass other creatures.

Obedience training will help your dog see you as the leader, so when you tell her "stop" and "leave it" she will be more likely to listen to you. During early training stages, keep your dog on a long leash so you can step on it when she starts chasing something. After halting her, get her to look at you and lure her back to your side with a treat and the "come" command. The goal is to elevate your status by calling the shots and providing her with a tasty reward that motivates her to come back to you.

Try to limit your dog's chase targets, especially if she has a dominant personality with a high prey drive. Keep her on a leash and harness when you walk through city parks where squirrels roam, or let her exercise inside the confines of a dog park where the squirrels are savvy enough not to be present.

Channel her chase drive in organized dog sports to allow her to safely follow her instincts. Try luring, in which canine teams are timed while they chase a mechanical, fast-moving object through a maze.

BEHAVIOR TYPES: **Aggressive** *p.178* • **Bored** *p.180* • **Predatory** *p.184*

# 45 Chasing Cars

○ Your Labrador Retriever bolts out the open gate to run after a car that passes by on the street.

○ Your dog drags you down the sidewalk during a walk because a car goes zooming by.

○ You pull into your driveway and your **Australian Shepherd** is hot on your tires, barking like crazy.

## BREEDS

- Australian Shepherd
- Border Collie
- English Pointer
- German Shepherd
- Labrador Retriever
- Pembroke Welsh Corgi
- Siberian Husky

**WHAT YOUR DOG WANTS**

Dogs chase cars for different reasons. Some have a strong hunting instinct, which prompts them to run after anything that moves. Most dogs who run after cars are not so much concerned about catching them as they are in the chase. However, there are some dogs who think they have a good chance of catching the car and "killing" it, as ridiculous as that seems.

Certain dogs see vehicles as intruders on their territory and want the offending hunk of metal out of sight. They try to get the big, noisy thing to leave the area by unleashing a bark barrage and dashing after it. Although no dog can outrun a moving car, in the dog's mind her actions have been successful. After all, the vehicle "flees" the scene, only reinforcing the dog's behavior.

Some dogs with herding instincts may view cars as runaway sheep that need to be brought back to the flock. Never mind that a Toyota has no resemblance to a woolly lamb. It is all the same to a herding dog.

 **VET'S NOTE**

> *Dogs who chase cars are engaging in a dangerous sport. This action can expose your dog to being hit or killed by other cars in the street.*

 **HOW TO RESPOND**

Your dog needs a way to burn off her energy and fulfill her strong chase drive. Start by spending time having her chase more appropriate objects, such as a ball. Take her to the backyard or a fenced dog park and throw the ball for her until she just cannot run anymore.

Training her to fetch is also a good way to channel her instincts for good. Get her in the habit of chasing things that she can bring back to you so you will throw them again. She cannot do this with a car, which means that racing after motorized vehicles may soon lose its appeal.

Teaching your dog to "come" when she is called is another great tool to stop her from chasing cars. If you see her go after a moving vehicle and she has what dog trainers call a "strong recall," you will be able to get her attention off the car and back on to you. To get this level of reliability from your dog, you need to practice getting her to come to you when called, regardless of distracting and/or exciting circumstances. Just because she comes when she is sitting around with nothing to do does not mean she will listen when she is in the middle of a hot vehicle pursuit.

BEHAVIOR TYPES: **Aggressive** *p.178* • **Bored** *p.180* • **Predatory** *p.184*

# 46 Burying Objects

○ Missing your TV remote? Check that fresh dirt mound in your backyard.

○ Be careful when you sit on the sofa—that lump you feel under the cushion may be your dog's toy or your toddler's doll.

○ One minute your watch is on the nightstand, and the next it has disappeared.

○ Dogs do not need bank safe-deposit boxes to protect their prized possessions. All they need is soft dirt or a pile of laundry.

## WHAT YOUR DOG WANTS

Your dog is following an ancestral urge. Thousands of years ago, roaming dogs did not know where their next meal would come from, so after a better-than-expected hunt, they buried surplus food to hide it from scavengers. When these dogs became hungry, they returned to the secret location and dug up their leftovers. Dirt also served as Mother Nature's refrigerator, keeping buried bones fresher longer by protecting them from sunlight. This natural "aging" made the bone tastier, too.

Have you been too generous with treats and toys? Your dog may simply be storing extras in a safe place to retrieve later and possibly share with canine visitors.

Some dogs cannot resist bling and are attracted to shiny objects, such as watches and earrings. They grab these items off counters and dash to a certain burying place, perhaps under the cushion in their dog bed or in the laundry basket.

Dogs often engage in this grab-and-hide behavior when they are lonely, bored, or seeking attention. They are not being mean or malicious—they hope their actions will garner playtime with you.

## HOW TO RESPOND

Dogs have long been advocates of the "save for a rainy day" mentality and their almighty noses faithfully guide them to just the place where they buried their treasures.

Pick up spare toys or dog bones. Limit your dog's access to one or two toys and stash the rest away. Rotate different toys. By limiting the quantity and providing variety, you may lessen your dog's strong urge to take her treasures out to the yard.

Indoors, direct her need to bury by teaching your dog to hide a favorite bone or toy under a blanket. Make it a fun game you play a few times a week. Strive to improve your dog's vocabulary understanding by having her correctly bury the right object.

## BREEDS

- Airedale
- Golden Retriever
- Labrador Retriever
- Manchester Terrier
- Miniature Schnauzer

## VET'S NOTE

> *The backyard marinating of an old bone may cause stomach upset or diarrhea in your dog. If this is the case, she needs vet care. Do not let your dog take edible items out to the backyard to bury for the sake of her health.*

BEHAVIOR TYPES: **Attention-seeking** *p.179* • **Bored** *p.180* • **Confident** *p.180* • **Happy** *p.182* • **Obsessive-Compulsive** *p.183* • **Predatory** *p.184*

# 47 Digging in Dirt

○ Watch your step—you might take an unexpected dip or trip while walking in your backyard.

○ Your yard looks like it hosted a gopher reunion.

○ Your Cairn Terrier cannot deny her digging deed—proof is found in the dirt under her nails as she proudly walks across your newly vacuumed carpet.

○ Digging is a clever canine way to combat the sizzling dog days of summer.

## BREEDS

- Basenji
- Border Collie
- Cairn Terrier
- Dachshund
- German Shepherd
- Glen of Imaal Terrier
- Labrador Retriever
- Norfolk Terrier
- Staffordshire Bull Terrier

## WHAT YOUR DOG WANTS

Terriers rank No. 1 in the dog-digging department. The name "terrier" is derived from the Latin word *terra*, which means earth. These dogs have been bred to hunt rabbits and other underground prey, so they dig with gusto to try to capture critters.

Digging fills some dogs with delight and a sense of accomplishment. Like a painter who can step back and admire his work on a house, a digging dog can sit back and admire the "depth" of her work.

Digging helps fend off boredom. This is the canine equivalent to people who knit or perform other keep-busy activities with their hands.

Hot dogs know how to keep cool. By digging dirt, they create shallow spots that fit their bodies. The lower layers of dirt are cooler in temperature than surface dirt. Dogs plop their bellies on the just-dug dirt as a canine version of air-conditioning.

## VET'S NOTE

> *Check your dog's paws and nails, especially if she tries digging in frozen turf or on rocks. She may suffer cuts in her feet and bleeding paw pads that need to be treated. A vet may need to give pain medication for deep wounds and bandage the injured paw.*
> *Dogs who excessively and destructively dig may need medication to address a serious obsessive-compulsive behavior.*

## HOW TO RESPOND

Digging holes in the backyard is a canine cry to chase away boredom. It is often a signal that your dog needs more activity in her day. It is time to shake things up and get out of your dull routine. Take her along to a dog-friendly beach and encourage your dog to dig in the sand. Praise her. Become her cheerleader and watch her proudly perform.

Digging can be a difficult habit for your dog to break, so strike a compromise. Fence your garden to protect it from being plowed over. Cover any undesired digging spots with chicken wire, bricks, or other objects that are not paw-friendly, but also provide your dog with a place in the backyard to dig to her heart's content. Place a plastic child's pool in a corner, fill it with sand, and stash some treats and toys in it for your dog to dig to find.

BEHAVIOR TYPES: **Attention-seeking** *p.179* • **Bored** *p.180* • **Obsessive-Compulsive** *p.183* • **Playful** *p.183*

# 48 Rolling in Smelly Objects

○ Your dog may be saying, "Hey, what do you mean you do not like my rotten-fish cologne?"

○ The rolling in duck "doo-doo" occurs precisely 15 minutes after you have bathed your dog.

○ Your dog, fresh from rolling in horse manure, rubs against your white pants and tries to give you a friendly body-hug with her front paws.

○ Your dog wants to demonstrate her new trick—it is called the dead-squirrel dance.

## BREEDS

• This action is not limited to specific breeds.

## WHAT YOUR DOG WANTS

Dogs roll in smelly stuff for many reasons, but the canine family tree tops the list. You can blame your dog's disgusting habit on her ancestors. This is an instinctive behavior that harks back to predomesticated days when "scout" dogs brought back information about available food to the rest of the pack. The reasoning was this: if they located decaying fish on their hunt, then fresher fish should not be far away.

Dogs also roll and wiggle in foul-smelling feces and decay to create a cunning olfactory disguise that bolsters their hunting opportunities. After all, what better way to sneak up on and catch a rabbit than to smell like one, even a dead one? Think of this maneuver as a form of canine camouflage.

Certain dogs detest the flowery scent that is found in some pet shampoos. Even though you love the smell of lavender, your Labrador Retriever may absolutely loathe it. At the first opportunity, your freshly bathed dog may head outside to find a way to remove the soapy smell, and what better way for her to do this than by rolling in a pile of rabbit poop or duck droppings?

## VET'S NOTE

> Dogs can be infected with parasites that reside in decaying animals and poop, especially if they not only roll in these objects but eat them, too. Make sure your dog's vaccinations and parasite-control medications are up-to-date.

## HOW TO RESPOND

Just be grateful that your own sense of smell is so far inferior to that of your dog's, otherwise her stinky coat would really leave you reeling. Select dog shampoos that are void of heavy scents— remember to honor your dog's stronger sense of smell. Consult with a professional groomer to find the right dog shampoo that best matches your dog's coat condition.

Be proactive on hikes and walks with your dog. Patrol the area in front of you for any possible "stink bombs," such as another dog's poop deposit or duck doo-doo. Keep your dog on a short leash so that you can stop her before she gets ready to plop in a poop pile. Always carry healthy treats with you to reward and encourage your dog when she stops and comes back to you.

Finally, practice the "leave it" command inside your home, then in your backyard. Build your dog's level of compliance with distractions before taking her on a hike or long walk.

# 49 Eating Grass

- Your dog's zeal for eating grass has earned her a nickname in the neighborhood: "Elsie the cow."

- All meat and no greens do not make for a balanced dog diet.

- Do not be tempted to sell your lawn mower—there is a limit to the safe amount of grass a dog can consume each day.

- Your dog's grass-eating ways serve as a gentle reminder for you to eat a garden salad or other source of healthy greens.

**WHAT YOUR DOG WANTS**

Just like us, dogs like variety in their daily cuisine. They also innately know the benefit of adding some greens to their meals. Put yourself in your dog's paws: would you be able to savor eating the same turkey sandwich every day of your life? It would get boring quickly. Dogs, by definition, are obligate omnivores. They benefit most from balanced diets that contain meat and vegetables.

Some dogs have a preference for grass. In this case, they simply like the taste and texture. These dogs will chew and swallow grass blades thoroughly.

Grass can be a wonderful health-aid for dogs that have upset stomachs or are suffering from nausea. Sometimes, when a dog feels the need to purge her stomach, she will quickly gobble grass without really chewing it. The prickly stalks of the grass blades will irritate her stomach lining and cause her to vomit, or the blades may intertwine with the food that is disagreeing with her and cause her to expel the food.

## VET'S NOTE

> *A vet may put a dog who is determined to eat a lot of grass on a high-fiber diet, to ensure the dog meets her daily nutritional needs.*

> *Dogs who eat grass may be tempted to dine on houseplants. Some houseplants, such as ivy, are poisonous to dogs. Contact your vet immediately if your dog has nibbled on plant leaves—or eaten grass treated with pesticides—and shows such signs as foaming at the mouth, vomiting, and/or diarrhea.*

 **HOW TO RESPOND**

If your dog is an ardent fan of grass consumption, make sure that her source of greens is free of pesticides, lawn chemicals, or other harmful substances. Make her day by growing a container of grass for her to nibble on indoors or grow a special patch of grass for her in your backyard, so she has a healthy source of fiber and chlorophyll.

Your dog's diet may lack certain vitamins, minerals, or fibers that are not found in protein. Add some cooked or raw vegetables to her diet, especially carrots or green beans, to fortify her meals.

Do not allow your dog to go overboard on her grass consumption, to the point that it becomes excessive. Too much of anything, even a good thing, is not healthy.

## BREEDS

- **This action is not limited to specific breeds.**

BEHAVIOR TYPES: **Bored** *p.180* • **Happy** *p.182* • **Obsessive-Compulsive** *p.183*

# 50 Eating Inedible Objects

- Uh-oh. There is a huge hole in your wool sweater and you see a bit of fabric dangling from your dog's mouth.

- You can no longer change channels using your TV remote because your dog ate half of it.

- Your dog shows more interest in begging to chew on the plastic grocery bag than eating the treats you bought for her that are contained within it.

## WHAT YOUR DOG WANTS

Your dog's bizarre eating preference is more often caused by behavioral or medical disorders than by nutritional problems.

It does not matter if the inedible object of desire consumed by your dog is a sock, sweater, plastic bag, gravel, rubber band, or other item. The act of eating inedible objects has a medical definition: pica. It is a serious condition that should not be ignored or allowed to progress.

Some puppies are particularly curious. They explore their environments by putting objects of interest in their mouths and sometimes chew and swallow them.

## VET'S NOTE

> Diabetes, hyperthyroidism, severe inflammatory bowel disease, stomach tumors, anemia, pancreatic insufficiency, and gastrointestinal conditions are among the top medical reasons for dogs eating inedible items.
> A vet will often perform diagnostic tests, including a complete blood count, urinalysis, and biochemical profile, to check the health of the organs and rule out other possible diseases.
> X-rays and endoscopic procedures may be necessary to identify the swallowed object and its location, which may require surgical removal.
> If the cause is obsessive-compulsiveness, a vet may prescribe Prozac and antidepressant medications. Behavior-modification training, under the supervision of a certified animal behaviorist, may also be warranted.

## HOW TO RESPOND

Show your dog how much you love her—and want to protect her—by becoming a neater housekeeper. Remove objects within reach that she could chew and swallow, or spray them with cayenne pepper, bitter apple, citronella, or other flavors your dog abhors. Store plastic grocery bags in a place inaccessible to your dog and patrol the yard for inedible temptations.

Keep your dog on a short leash during walks to prevent her from eating rocks and feces. Divert her attention using treats or by having her perform a trick on cue.

Provide safe chew toys and encourage her to play with them by heaping on plenty of praise.

Some dogs act this way out of boredom or for attention. Exercise and play with your dog daily.

## BREEDS

- German Shepherd
- Golden Retriever
- Labrador Retriever
- Poodle
- Schnauzer

BEHAVIOR TYPES: Anxious/Stressed *p.179* • Attention-seeking *p.179* • Bored *p.180* • Curious *p.181* • Obsessive-Compulsive *p.183*

# 51 Raiding the Litter Box

- Your dog regards the cat's litter box as an all-you-can-eat smorgasbord open 24 hours, seven days a week.

- There is a reason the time it takes to scoop the litter box has decreased since you adopted your dog.

- After snacking from the litter box, your triumphant dog heads your way to give you a big kiss. Yuck!

## BREEDS

- This action is not limited to specific breeds.

**WHAT YOUR DOG WANTS**

Canine raiding of cat stools covered in litter has a scientific name: coprophagy (stool eating). No matter the name, this action makes people feel horrified and downright disgusted.

One of the key reasons that dogs resort to eating stools is a vitamin deficiency in their diets. The food your dog presently consumes may be too low in protein, fiber, or fat, or it may have inadequate vitamin B levels.

You can also blame your dog's heritage. Before human intervention, female dogs would eat their puppies' stools in order to keep their dens clean and thereby make them less likely to attract the attention of potential predators.

For some dogs, raiding the litter box boils down to taste. Remember, your dog's palate differs greatly from yours. Cat food is high in protein and often more aromatic than dog food. Consequently, the stools in the litter box yield a strong aroma that some dogs just cannot resist.

Other dogs do this deed because they are bored and looking for something to spice up their mundane day. "Hunting" for cat stools may be one of your dog's favorite pastimes to relieve her boredom.

**VET'S NOTE**

❯ *Work with your vet on selecting dog food that is higher in protein and contains more vitamins, so that you can provide a balanced diet for your dog.*

 **HOW TO RESPOND**

It is important to provide your cat with a safe, private place to eliminate—away from your stool-seeking canine. Place a dog gate in the door of the room where the litter box is located, so your agile cat can leap up and over, but your dog's path is blocked. Alternatively, locate the litter box on a counter or sturdy shelf that your dog cannot reach, or use hooded litter boxes that your medium- to large-sized dog cannot enter.

Step up your "poop patrol" by scooping the litter box out more frequently.

However, you cannot stand guard by the cat's litter box every moment of every day, so sprinkle some pancreatic enzymes over the litter. Available at pet supply stores, these enzymes will cause the stools to taste unpleasant to your dog. Just make sure that the additive used does not also cause your cat to start boycotting the litter box.

BEHAVIOR TYPES: **Bored** *p.180* • **Curious** *p.181*

# 52 Raiding the Garbage

○ One man's trash is a dog's dining treasure. It is all just a matter of perspective.

○ Your dog may mistakenly view the kitchen trash can as a canine all-you-can-eat buffet.

○ Discarded human food outranks that ho-hum-tasting dry kibble found in your dog's bowl.

○ Some human thieves steal jewelry— canine thieves steal food.

## BREEDS

- Basset Hound
- Beagle
- Bulldog
- Labrador Retriever
- Staffordshire Bull Terrier

## WHAT YOUR DOG WANTS

Much like the motivation of seasoned mountain climbers about to ascend another lofty peak, dogs will rummage through the kitchen trash can because it is there and because you are not. They also view it as easy pickings for delicious food treats.

Some dogs do not know household rules and need to be properly trained on acceptable behaviors. This especially applies to puppies or newly adopted shelter dogs.

Dogs who are not fed on any kind of regular schedule—or worse, who you have forgotten to feed—use their canine survival instincts to sniff out a food source. Just like you, dogs do best when fed two or three meals a day.

## VET'S NOTE

> If your dog seems to be constantly hungry and on the hunt for more food, consult your vet about switching to a diet that better suits her needs without resulting in excess calorie intake.

> Garbage consumption can cause diarrhea and vomiting, and may require vet care. Dogs may cut their paws or tongues on can lids and require stitches. They can also choke on chicken or turkey bones, or swallow bone splinters that require surgical removal.

## HOW TO RESPOND

Take away this temptation by placing your kitchen trash can in a pantry with a closed door or behind a dog gate, or replace your easy-to-break-into can with one that features a sturdy, dog-proof lid.

Make it a habit to always remove the kitchen trash when it contains chicken bones or other canine temptations, and deposit it in an outside receptacle.

You can "booby trap" your trash can to make it less appealing by placing a commercial deterrent nearby. These motion-activated devices trigger a blast of compressed air when a dog gets within range. You can also purchase a sheet of plastic that gives a mild static charge when a dog steps on it. Neither of these devices will harm your dog.

Reinforce the "leave it" command with your dog on a regular basis, so that she knows her boundaries.

When your dog starts to head to the trash can, divert her attention by providing her with a chew toy, hollow synthetic bone, or hollow hard-rubber toy that you have stuffed with peanut butter or cheese.

Take your bored dog on adventure-filled walks and provide her with dog-food puzzles to garner her interest. She needs to be mentally and physically challenged on a daily basis.

BEHAVIOR TYPES: **Attention-seeking** *p.179* • **Bored** *p.180* • **Curious** *p.181* • **Dominant** *p.181*

# 53 Spilling Water from Bowls

- Maybe your dog observed you washing the floor and wants to lend a helping paw?

- You did not realize that bowls are just asking to be tipped over.

- Even though you are frustrated at having to mop up the water on the floor, you are grateful that it is from the bowl and not from your dog's behind.

 **WHAT YOUR DOG WANTS**

Some dogs take to water like ducks. These dogs enjoy establishing an aqua playground right on your kitchen floor. They are trying to create fun games to fend off boredom or to catch your attention.

Certain water-loving breeds, such as the various retrievers, like to feel cool water on their paw pads and want to make a splash—literally.

Fast-growing puppies put the capital "C" in curious and look for ways to use all the senses to explore their environments, especially the sense of touch.

### BREEDS

- Chesapeake Bay Retriever
- Golden Retriever
- Labrador Retriever

### VET'S NOTE

> *No specific medical advice for this action.*

 **HOW TO RESPOND**

Replace those easy-to-spill bowls with ones that feature spill-proof bottoms. This will save you time sopping up water and money buying paper towels.

Put the bowl on a large plastic mat with sides, to keep spills from reaching the floor.

Make sure new bowls can be cleaned in a dishwasher, or replace bowls altogether with a heavy-duty, automatic pet water fountain.

BEHAVIOR TYPES: **Attention-seeking** *p.179* • **Bored** *p.180* • **Curious** *p.181*

# 54 Eating Feces

- You look out the window to find your dog nibbling on her own excrement.

- Your dog likes to wander onto the neighbor's property and eat her rabbits' droppings.

## BREEDS

- Dalmatian
- French Bulldog
- Poodle
- Shetland Sheepdog

## VET'S NOTE

> Dogs do not seem to be harmed by ingesting feces, although they may need more frequent deworming if they are fanatical about this action.

> Dogs who eat bird feces are at risk of being infected with giardia, which is a potentially debilitating intestinal parasite.

## WHAT YOUR DOG WANTS

Although we find this habit disgusting, it is acceptable among dogs. It may stem from the fact that a mother dog eats her puppies' stools to keep the den clean, but full-grown male dogs are still among the culprits.

Dogs like to satisfy their palates just like humans. But, unlike humans, some dogs think poop is yummy.

Others eat feces because they lack adequate levels of protein in their commercial dog-food diets.

## HOW TO RESPOND

More dogs than we would care to mention snack on the stools of other animals, such as horses, deer, and rabbits. And, yes, some even eat their own deposits.

Discourage this behavior by quickly picking up excrement so your dog does not have access to it. If she likes eating poop from other animals, preventing her from getting at it may be your only recourse.

BEHAVIOR TYPES: Bored p.180

# 55 House Soiling

- You regularly find puddles of urine on the floor in the house.

- When you come home from work, you know you will be picking up dog poop in the living room.

- You cannot take your dog to your friends' homes because she will pee on their furniture.

- As soon as you walk in the front door, your dog squats and pees in front of you.

## BREEDS

- American Staffordshire Terrier
- Basset Hound
- Bichon Frise
- Boxer
- Cocker Spaniel
- Pomeranian
- West Highland White Terrier
- Whippet

## WHAT YOUR DOG WANTS

Your dog may be house soiling for a number of reasons. She may not have developed the habit of going outside to urinate and defecate. This is something that is best taught to a dog when she is a puppy. Dogs who have been kept outside a lot, or have been confined for long periods of time to a kennel or crate, may never have learned that it is not acceptable to go to the bathroom inside the house.

Some dogs soil the house because another dog has already urinated on the rug or furniture, and the dog smells it. In response, they urinate on the area to reclaim their turf. Unaltered dogs may urinate indoors to mark their territory.

Dogs who are sick can start soiling the house because they do not feel well. This is usually the case when a reliably housebroken dog starts eliminating in the house without an obvious reason.

## VET'S NOTE

> House soiling can be a sign of serious illness. If the cause of your dog's behavior is not readily obvious, take her to the vet for a checkup.

 ## HOW TO RESPOND

If a dog has not developed the habit of going to the bathroom outside, she will relieve herself wherever she happens to be when the urge hits her.

In some cases, dogs soil the house in order to mark their territory. Removing all traces of urine by using a product designed to remove urine odors is the best way to eliminate this problem.

Dogs who are house soiling need to start "Housetraining 101." They must be taught that the only acceptable place to urinate and defecate is outdoors. If your dog has not been overly restricted to a crate, you can use this tool to teach her to "hold it" inside the house by keeping her confined in the crate when she is indoors, and taking her outside frequently to relieve herself. You can graduate to keeping her in an exercise pen or small room until she is completely reliable at going to the bathroom outside.

Train apartment-dwelling dogs, or dogs who must stay indoors for longer than eight hours, to use commercially made synthetic patches of grass. These products contain safe scent chemicals that beckon a dog to use this "indoor" bathroom, and are easy to keep clean and free of odors.

If a dog is not feeling well or is having trouble controlling her bowels or bladder, she may soil the house.

BEHAVIOR TYPES: Anxious/Stressed p.179 • Dominant p.181 • Sad p.184 • Sexual p.185

# 56 Drinking from Toilet Bowl

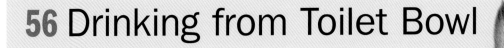

o  Your dog may be thinking, "Wow, this house has not
   one but two dog water fountains. I am one lucky dog!"

o  Attention gentlemen, if you need another reason to put
   the lid down after use, think of your dog wanting to
   kiss you after she makes a drink run in the bathroom.

o  Water tends to stay cooler in the toilet bowl than
   in the stainless steel water bowl in the kitchen.

o  Toilet bowls are the perfect height for large-
   to giant-breed dogs to quench their thirsts.

### BREEDS

- Bernese Mountain Dog
- English Springer Spaniel
- German Shepherd
- German Shorthaired Pointer
- Labrador Retriever

## WHAT YOUR DOG WANTS

Your beverage of choice may be a French merlot or a freshly squeezed orange juice served in a frosted glass, but to dogs the eau de toilet is viewed as canine champagne. Water in toilet bowls is cooler and fresher than stale water that lingers all day in a dog's bowl. With each flush of the toilet, a fresh supply of water enters the toilet bowl. From a dog's viewpoint, this sure beats drinking sidewalk puddles to quench a thirst.

Your dog's partiality for fresh water is nothing new. Her ancestors preferred to drink running water found in streams, over water in stagnant pools, because it was better aerated.

Porcelain keeps water tasting like, well, pure water. Dog water bowls that are made of plastic or stainless steel can change the way water tastes to a thirsty dog and make drinking from these vessels less appealing. Remember, dogs have discerning noses.

Do not overlook the flooring that is common in bathrooms. Floors in bathrooms tend to be made of tile or other smooth coverings that are cool to paw pads and provide a refreshing place for your dog to nap on a hot day.

## VET'S NOTE

> *Chemicals used to clean bacteria in toilet bowls can be toxic if swallowed by your dog. Contact a vet immediately in the event of accidental poisoning.*

 ## HOW TO RESPOND

The easiest solution takes two seconds: keep the toilet lid down. You may need to post a friendly reminder above the toilet for other members of your home and guests, so you can help break this undesired habit in your dog.

Treat your dog to clean, bottled water served with ice cubes in porcelain bowls that you wash daily. Locate these bowls in cool places, out of direct sunlight and away from floor heaters.

Provide a canine drinking fountain that operates on batteries or plugs into an outlet. These fountains entice dogs with flowing water. Just remember that you need to change the filter in drinking fountains as instructed to keep the water fresh.

Some pet manufacturers make vitamin-enriched water that comes in chicken, liver, lamb, and beef flavors. These flavors can motivate dogs to drink adequate amounts of water and avoid dehydration.

BEHAVIOR TYPES: **Confident** *p.180* • **Curious** *p.181*

# 57 Circling Before Sleeping

○ You may get dizzy watching your dog make tight, clockwise circles before each nap.

○ Your dog performs *Goldilocks and the Three Bears*, circling until the bed is just right.

## BREEDS

• This action is not limited to specific breeds.

 **WHAT YOUR DOG WANTS**

Even though most dogs enjoy the indoor pampered life, with plenty of comfy napping spots in the house, they still retain the nesting instinct that has prevailed in dogs for countless generations. Circling and pawing the bed are the same actions that your dog's ancestors made when they circled and pawed at twigs and leaves to create just the right bowl shape to fit their bodies for a nap.

Circling also releases your dog's scent. It is the aromatic alert to other dogs that this bed belongs to her, and her alone.

 **HOW TO RESPOND**

Try not to draw a lot of attention to your dog when she begins her circling ritual, or you may inadvertently encourage her to perform as a way to garner your attention and affection.

Make sure you provide your dog with a canine bed that fits her size and provides orthopedic foam support for her joints.

## VET'S NOTE

> *This is a harmless activity that requires no medical intervention, except in extreme circumstances when your dog circles constantly to the point of ignoring food or sleeping. In this case, she needs antianxiety medications.*

BEHAVIOR TYPES: **Anxious/Stressed** *p.179* • **Attention-seeking** *p.179* • **Confident** *p.180* • **Dominant** *p.181* • **Obsessive-Compulsive** *p.183*

# 58 Denning inside Crate

○ Your dog was an interior designer in a previous life.

○ The crate may seem small compared to the size of your bedroom, but it feels just the right, cozy size to your dog.

## BREEDS

• This action is not limited to specific breeds.

## VET'S NOTE

➤ *Nervous dogs or those coping with separation anxiety may feel more at home in their crate if you plug a dog-appeasing pheromone unit into a nearby outlet. Ask your vet for a recommendation for this over-the-counter product. Antianxiety medication may be prescribed in extreme situations.*

## WHAT YOUR DOG WANTS

When humans move into a new place, we do things to make it feel like home. Dogs are no different. They fuss and paw at items in their crates and do a little rearranging as a way to claim their crates as their own canine condos.

Your dog may shred her bedding to add a little more fluffiness and make things more comfortable, or she may feel bored inside her closed crate while you are gone and is denning to pass the time.

## HOW TO RESPOND

Take steps to improve the way your dog perceives the real-estate value of her crate by providing her with a cushiony floor pad, a favorite chew toy, and a non-spill water bowl.

Locate the crate in a place that your dog feels safe and able to easily survey her surroundings.

Never force your dog into her crate or usher her in as a punishment. Both you and your dog should regard her crate as a positive, safe place.

BEHAVIOR TYPES: **Attention-seeking** *p.179* • **Bored** *p.180* • **Confident** *p.180* • **Dominant** *p.181* • **Happy** *p.182* • **Obsessive-Compulsive** *p.183*

# 59 Pacing during Storms

○ Your usually obedient dog does not listen to your cues to "sit" or "stay."

○ Before the first clap of thunder, your quivering dog cowers in the bathtub.

○ Desperate to escape a thunderstorm, your frightened dog bolts through the front door, or worse, tries to crash through a window.

○ Some food-motivated dogs decline even their most favorite treats during a thunderstorm.

**BREEDS**

- Australian Kelpie
- Australian Shepherd
- Bearded Collie
- Border Collie
- Golden Retriever
- Great Pyrenees
- Labrador Retriever
- Whippet

## ? WHAT YOUR DOG WANTS

Mother Nature's ugly side—clapping thunder and lightning streaking across a dark sky—can transform even the largest dogs into frightened little Fidos. Dogs can sense the electricity in the air and smell the changes in barometric pressure.

As the storm approaches and during the storm, thunderstorm-phobic dogs often pace continuously, pant, and may even urinate or defecate. They may also hide, try to escape, drool, seek your comfort, lose their appetite, ignore commands, have dilated pupils, bark repetitively, or whine.

Fear of storms is more common in dogs than people realize. Often a dog shows signs of storm phobia by age two, and, left unchecked, her fear intensifies.

## VET'S NOTE

> Storm phobia is serious. It requires medication and a behavior-modification program outlined by a vet, perhaps in partnership with an animal behaviorist.

> Amitriptyline, fluoxetine, buspirone, or diazepam is often prescribed. Vet studies have shown that melatonin is also effective in calming dogs.

> You may never rid your dog of storm fear, but you can manage it more effectively.

## ✓ HOW TO RESPOND

Do not ever physically hit or yell at your frightened dog. Remember, a phobia is an irrational response to a perceived threat. Punishing your dog for her fearful behavior will only worsen her response to the sight, sound, and barometric pressure that is unleashed by a thunderstorm.

Do not cuddle or try to comfort your quivering canine by petting her or consoling her with baby talk. Although well meant, these actions will inadvertently validate that your dog should be scared of storms.

Divert her attention with a favorite indoor game, grooming, or other activity that she likes. When you know a storm is forecast, increase your dog's exercise a few hours prior to the storm. Her natural serotonin levels will be boosted by the exercise and can act as a sedative.

Consider using calming products, such as blends of specific calming flower essences, dog-appeasing pheromones, music therapy—particularly harp music—and body-wrapping clothing, which may all help to sooth your frightened dog.

Other effective strategies include running a fan or turning on the television to create white noise and block out the thunderstorm's sounds. Dogs are denning animals; during a thunderstorm, some dogs feel calmer inside their crate, placed in a bathroom with the fan turned on.

BEHAVIOR TYPES: Anxious/Stressed p.179 • Fearful p.182

# 60 Hiking Up Leg to Urinate

○ It takes forever to walk your dog because he has to stop and lift his leg at every tree.

○ Your dog seems to aim higher when he lifts his leg on some objects than others.

## BREEDS

- Bull Terrier
- German Shepherd
- Labrador Retriever
- Schnauzer
- Yorkshire Terrier

## WHAT YOUR DOG WANTS

Leg-lifting to mark territory with urine is the favorite pastime of most male dogs, whether they are neutered or not. Although it can be an annoying habit—especially when you are walking your dog—leaving his calling card is something your dog enjoys.

Lifting a leg when urinating allows a dog to aim at nose level. Other dogs are more likely to detect a whiff of his urine when they happen by because your dog took the trouble to leave his mark high.

## HOW TO RESPOND

If your dog makes your walks unbearable because he has to stop at every tree, allocate the first part of the walk to urinating on objects and the second part to brisk walking with no stops.

### VET'S NOTE

> Unaltered male dogs are more likely to frequently lift their legs when urinating. Neutering them can reduce this behavior, although it will not be completely eliminated.

BEHAVIOR TYPES: Confident *p.180* • Dominant *p.181* • Sexual *p.185*

# 61 Shredding Paper

- You come home to find the novel you are reading torn to pieces.

- When your son says the dog ate his homework, he is not lying.

## BREEDS

- American Eskimo Dog
- Boxer
- Cairn Terrier
- Fox Terrier
- Golden Retriever
- Maltese

 ## WHAT YOUR DOG WANTS

Many dogs like to tear things up. Shredding paper is great fun for dogs and they do not see the harm in it, especially as it provides an outlet for their energy.

Some dogs simply enjoy the sensation of tearing something with their mouths, much like they would tear at their prey if they were hunting in the wild.

Other dogs shred paper when they feel bored, stressed, or anxious.

 ## HOW TO RESPOND

To help your dog get off her paper-shredding habit, avoid leaving paper around and provide her with an alternative item to occupy her mouth, such as a chew toy.

A hollow, hard-rubber toy is one of the best objects that you can offer your mouthy dog. Fill the toy with peanut butter or processed cheese spread, then watch as your dog spends time and energy on working out how to remove the food.

## VET'S NOTE

> *Dogs who swallow paper can develop digestive problems. Swallowing a large amount of paper can cause an intestinal blockage.*

BEHAVIOR TYPES: Anxious/Stressed *p.179* • Bored *p.180*

# 62 Placing Head over a Dog

○ Think of this action as the canine equivalent of two people moving their hands up a baseball bat to determine who gets to bat first.

○ Your confident Siberian Husky struts up to the Miniature Schnauzer at the dog park and places his head over the Schnauzer's back without uttering a single bark.

○ When your adult Labrador Retriever plays with another dog, he tries to put his head on the other dog's back. Not wanting to be dominated, the other dog responds by wiggling out from underneath him.

## BREEDS

- Alaskan Malamute
- Bouvier des Flandres
- Bull Terrier
- Labrador Retriever
- Rottweiler
- Siberian Husky
- West Highland White Terrier

## WHAT YOUR DOG WANTS

When a dog places his head over another dog's neck, shoulders, or back, he is often displaying an attitude of dominance over that dog. Your dog wants the other dog to recognize his authority and to respond to it with submissive behavior.

The message your dog wants to convey is: "I am the boss of you. Do what I say, and there will not be any trouble." The other dog understands exactly what your dog is telling him and will answer by either accepting your dog's dominance or challenging him.

Some dogs act this way when they want to play with another dog. It's their version of commencing a playful romp, a desire to chase or to be chased. The other dog usually reacts by trying to get out from under the posturing dog. In this case, it is all-in fun. Dogs who are friends know the difference between the play form of this action and the alternative one that says: "I mean business."

## VET'S NOTE

> *A fight between dogs can result in serious bites and other injuries. Such unwelcome behavior can also solidify a dog's dominant attitude and render his "victims" more fearful and anxious.*

> *Some dogs can be emotionally scarred after being injured in a dogfight and may need calming medication from a vet.*

## HOW TO RESPOND

Keep a close eye on your dog when he socializes. Dogs who like to assert their dominance are at greater risk of being involved in a scuffle than dogs who prefer to communicate that they are submissive. In the canine world, dogs who act like bullies are not well received. Sooner or later, one of the dogs who your dog tries to dominate will call his bluff and growl or bite back.

If your dog lays his head over the back of the wrong dog, look out! Dogs rely on consistent postures and sounds in assessing each other's intentions and emotional state during introductions. Proceed with caution when your canine companion is around other dogs, but do not act fearful, scream, or yell. If you display these emotions, or make these vocalizations, you are only likely to trigger aggressive behavior from your dog.

Use a harness to limit your reactive dog's ability to lunge at other dogs, and keep his aggressive tendencies in check by not taking him to parks where you do not know the other dogs. Instead, let him play with a chosen few canine friends.

# 63 Front Pawing

○ Your dog may be saying, "Ahem, why did you stop scratching under my chin? I am still enjoying it."

○ Two Boxers in play look like they are performing the popular children's game of patty cake.

## BREEDS

- Bichon Frise
- Boxer
- Cairn Terrier
- Jack (Parson) Russell Terrier
- Norwich Terrier
- Yorkshire Terrier

## VET'S NOTE

› No specific medical advice for this action.

## ? WHAT YOUR DOG WANTS

Certain breeds, especially Boxers, have the special talent of being able to balance themselves on their hind legs and move their front paws in side-to-side and circular motions, much like a prize fighter does with his fists in the boxing ring. Their ability to stand up while battling opponents earned them the "boxer" name when this breed was developed in Germany in the nineteenth century.

Small and toy breeds, particularly Bichon Frises and Yorkshire Terriers, use front pawing as a way to spar during play and may even sneeze in excitement.

Digging breeds, such as Cairn and Jack (Parson) Russell Terriers, work vigorously as a team, using their front paws to dig for gophers and rabbits hiding in holes below ground.

## ✓ HOW TO RESPOND

Tap into your dog's front paw talents with special training and reward him with treats. Instead of the ordinary "shake a paw" cue, teach your dog to first shake with the left paw, then the right paw, and finish with a two-paw high five as a greeting.

BEHAVIOR TYPES: Affectionate p.178 • Attention-seeking p.179 • Dominant p.181 • Happy p.182 • Playful p.183

# 64 Urinating on a Dog's Urine

- Your dog is in the backyard with your aunt's dog and insists on peeing in the exact same spot as the other dog.

- He stops at every tree on your walk to pee where other neighborhood dogs urinated.

- Your dog got peed on when he got too close to a taller dog peeing on the same spot.

## BREEDS

- Cavalier King Charles Spaniel
- Collie
- Jack (Parson) Russell Terrier
- Miniature Pinscher
- Rhodesian Ridgeback
- Siberian Husky

## WHAT YOUR DOG WANTS

Dogs who urinate on the same spot as another dog are doing what is known as "over marking." The experts have different theories as to why dogs do this. One is that the over-marking dog is trying to cover the scent of the other dog's pee. Another theory is that the dog is expressing his dominance by peeing in the same spot.

This behavior is more common in male dogs, although female dogs have been known to do it, too.

## HOW TO RESPOND

This action is one that some dogs seem to enjoy, even though humans have not figured out why they do it.

Dogs have such a superior sense of smell than we do that they can pinpoint exactly where another dog has urinated, even when the pee has dried or is in the middle of a meadow.

## VET'S NOTE

> Unvaccinated puppies are at risk of contracting contagious diseases when they visit urination areas frequented by other dogs.

BEHAVIOR TYPES: **Dominant** *p.181* • **Sexual** *p.185*

# 65 Sniffing in Introductions

O Sniffs to the head and rear of another dog tell the sniffer so much more than merely touching front paws.

O People can fabricate a fake driver's license, but dogs cannot disguise their true identities from each other.

O Your friendly Beagle may be saying to the Poodle he just met, "Sniff, sniff. I see that you enjoyed breakfast today, with a side of turkey bacon."

### VET'S NOTE

> Bring your dog to a vet if another dog has bitten him. The wound on the skin's surface may look minor, but more severe tissue damage may have occurred beneath.

## ? WHAT YOUR DOG WANTS

While the idea of smelling urine, feces, and saliva may disgust people, those three bodily fluids top the popularity chart among dogs. During introductions, dogs download a lot of data about one another from the sniff-and-greet. They can obtain information as to the other dog's age, health condition, emotional state (happy, tired, stressed), sexual status (intact, neutered), and even what the other dog ate recently, down to the last piece of chicken-flavored kibble he consumed.

Dogs emit the strongest smells from the mouth, genitals, and anus. That explains why the first dog, usually the more dominant or confident one, will "check under the hood" and sniff the genitals and anus area of the second, less confident dog. This order also establishes social ranking between the two dogs.

### BREEDS

- **This action is not limited to specific breeds.**

## ✓ HOW TO RESPOND

Make this a happy and safe greeting by introducing the two dogs in a neutral place, so neither dog feels the need to be territorial. Instead of meeting in your backyard, have the two dogs meet at a dog park.

Be cognizant of how you handle the leash. Dogs are stellar at picking up on your emotions. If you rush to rein in your dog as another leashed dog approaches and keep a tight grip on the leash, your dog may infer that you are getting prepared for a fight. Instead of being friendly to the other dog, he may feel the need to defend you and act aggressively. Also, do not allow the leashes to become tangled.

Let the two dogs decide which one sniffs first. You may think your dog ranks higher, but the two dogs will be better able to make that call.

End the introduction before a problem surfaces. Calmly increase the distance between dogs if one engages in a non-blinking stare, leans stiffly forward on his front toes, places his head over the back of the other dog, curls his upper lip, or makes any other aggressive posture. It is only a matter of seconds before this dog snarls and lunges. Some dogs may even bite a dog that forces an unwanted introduction.

BEHAVIOR TYPES: **Affectionate** *p.178* • **Confident** *p.180* • **Curious** *p.181* • **Dominant** *p.181* • **Playful** *p.183* • **Sexual** *p.185*

# 66 Licking a Dog's Muzzle

- "No need for a tissue," your Cairn Terrier conveys as he licks away dripping drool from a Bull Mastiff.

- A newborn puppy licks the lips of his mother to let her know that he is hungry for her milk.

- An admiring Afghan Hound delivers a "salute" of respect to a brave Bernese Mountain Dog who just protected her from a canine bully at the local park.

## BREEDS

- Afghan Hound
- Bichon Frise
- Cairn Terrier
- Cavalier King Charles Spaniel
- Cocker Spaniel
- Maltese
- Newfoundland
- Weimaraner

## WHAT YOUR DOG WANTS

During an introduction, a timid and lower-ranking dog will lower his head, avoid direct eye contact, and gently extend his tongue to lick the muzzle of a more dominant, confident, and higher-ranking dog. The first dog licks the muzzle of the second dog to simply reconfirm that he comes in peace.

When puppies make the transition from suckling their mother's tits for milk to eating semisolid food, they vigorously lick their mother's muzzle in the hope of getting her to regurgitate some semidigested food for them.

Two strongly bonded canine pals will lick and groom one another. They give each other "dog kisses" in displays of affection and friendship. In this scenario, the dogs' social hierarchy is not an issue. These dogs know and trust one another.

## VET'S NOTE

> *Follow your vet's guidelines if you have a dog nursing a litter of puppies, to ensure that the puppies are getting the proper nutrition and that you know when and how to make the switch from their mother's milk to puppy food.*

> *A dog who excessively licks the muzzle of his canine pal may be doing this because the dog has a tumor, cut, or other medical need that requires attention and treatment.*

## HOW TO RESPOND

Carefully select confident-but-friendly and patient-tempered dogs to play with your shy dog, to help him hone his social skills. Also, consider enrolling him in a special training class that focuses on socialization, taught by an instructor who is certified in, and practices, positive training techniques.

Do not interfere when your two dogs play "kissy face" briefly with one another. Sit back and enjoy this display of canine friendship. Then call them over and have them do a command such as "sit" or "shake paws." Offer them treats simultaneously as a reward for being good to one another.

If you foster a dog and have three or more resident dogs, introduce the foster dog to your brood one dog at a time and let muzzle-licking between them happen naturally. Start with your least reactive or most friendly dog. Never force an introduction between the dogs because this can deepen the foster dog's submissiveness or spark a fight.

# 67 Humping or Mounting

○ Whenever your dog meets another dog, he jumps on top of the other dog and pins her with a full body tackle.

○ Your Yorkshire Terrier wraps himself tightly around the legs of all your guests as soon as they enter the door, then starts merrily humping away.

○ Watching your dog get personal with the sofa pillow makes you cringe—or gives you the urge to lower the lights and play some Barry White music for his benefit.

## BREEDS

- Bull Terrier
- Coonhound
- German Shorthaired Pointer
- Labrador Retriever
- Norwich Terrier
- Smooth Collie
- Standard Schnauzer
- Yorkshire Terrier

**WHAT YOUR DOG WANTS**

Dogs hump or mount other dogs, inanimate objects, and even people, to express their dominance or to release sexual energy. When a neutered male or spayed female mounts another dog, he or she is trying to say, "I am dominant over you." The other dog can allow the mounting or turn around and lash out.

The humping of pillows, blankets, toys, and other objects is sexual in nature and takes place when a male dog does not have a female to breed with. Unneutered males are riddled with testosterone, which results in a strong urge to mate. If they do not have a normal outlet for this desire, they will find a substitute and may develop an obsession with whatever they have chosen as the object of their lust.

 **HOW TO RESPOND**

Male dogs who have not been neutered are always on the lookout for romance, and, in the absence of a female, will substitute another male, a spayed female, your leg, or a pillow as their object of desire. Unless you are using these dogs as part of a responsible breeding program, they should be neutered to help curb their wanton urges.

Consider "sacrificing" a pillow or stuffed toy for your dog to relieve his need to hump, so he will have an acceptable object and be less likely to perform this habit on the household. Praise him for his actions on this targeted pillow and place it in his dog bed—and off the sofa.

If your poor dog is the target of humping, teach him some defensive postures, such as sitting, to curb mount-minded canines. Use treats to train your dog to get into the "parked" posture quickly, by having him sit down when you see the humping dog head your way. Indoors, you can deftly position your dog to sit with his back to a corner to block access from the rear.

 **VET'S NOTE**

> *Intact male dogs are at risk of certain health problems, including prostate enlargement, prostate cancer, testicular cancer, and peri-anal tumors.*

BEHAVIOR TYPES: **Aggressive** *p.178* • **Attention-seeking** *p.179* • **Dominant** *p.181* • **Sexual** *p.185*

# 68 Lunging on Leash

○ Your dog nearly pulls you off your feet when he sees another dog on a walk.

○ Your children are afraid to walk your dog because they end up being dragged along behind him.

○ Your dog spends much of his walk coughing after having lunged toward another dog and being choked by his collar.

## VET'S NOTE

› Dogs who continuously lunge on the leash are at risk of trachea damage. Small dogs are particularly susceptible.

## BREEDS

- Australian Shepherd
- Chow Chow
- English Springer Spaniel
- Great Dane
- Labrador Retriever
- Yorkshire Terrier

**WHAT YOUR DOG WANTS**

Your dog gets excited seeing other dogs when he is out on his walk and wants to make contact with them. His actions may be friendly or they might be aggressive. You can usually tell the difference if you look at other aspects of his posture. He may feel defensive because he perceives the other dog is invading his territory, which may be the actual neighborhood or you, the human at the end of his leash.

If your dog's hackles are raised, he is barking aggressively, and his teeth are showing, he is most likely lunging in an attempt to attack the other dog. The other dog's reaction can also be a clue. If the other dog returns the behavior, or instead cowers or shows another submissive behavior, such as a tucked tail, your dog is probably communicating aggression.

Your dog may also be excited because he wants to play with the other dog. Puppies are usually the ones who lunge on the leash because they are looking for fun. A puppy looking for a playmate has his ears down, wiggles, and yaps with excitement as he pulls on your arm to reach the other dog. He lunges in impatience because he wants to engage in playful romping—now!

 **HOW TO RESPOND**

Whether your dog lunges toward another dog to fight with him or to play with him, the remedy is the same: leash training.

On walks, your dog needs to view you as his leader and he should take his cues from you. It is best to start training proper leash walking when your dog is a puppy, so you can set him up for success. But you can also stop bad lunging habits in older dogs who you adopt from shelters.

Use a short leash during training, rather than a long or retractable one, so you have better control over your dog and can limit his range. Command your dog to "sit" and "watch me" while you have a friend with a well-socialized dog walk past you. Reward your dog for not lunging and for obeying you. Build on each success.

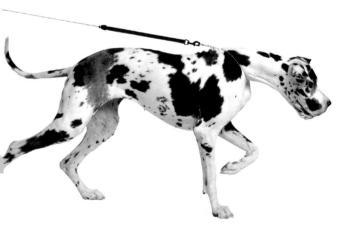

BEHAVIOR TYPES: **Confident** *p.180* • **Curious** *p.181* • **Dominant** *p.181* • **Happy** *p.182* • **Playful** *p.183*

# 69 Body Slamming

○ Welcome to dodge ball, canine-style. Who needs a ball when a muscular, fast-moving torso scores points?

○ An overzealous Bull Terrier accidentally "punts" his Cairn Terrier pal airborne during play with a full body-slam maneuver.

○ That strong, energetic Boxer was never taught how to reel back his body-wiggling enthusiasm.

**BREEDS**

- American Bulldog
- American Staffordshire Terrier
- Boxer
- Bull Terrier
- Labrador Retriever

**WHAT YOUR DOG WANTS**

With more than 180 different dog breeds, diversity rules in size and temperament. There are some dogs who prefer to play quietly or to embark on a quest to find an available lap in which to take a nap. There are dogs who like to stay on the sidelines, along the fence at dog parks, and "bark-bark-bark" like cheerleaders. Then there are other dogs who cannot think of anything better than unleashed, rough, body-slamming play.

Many bully breeds naturally move their torso in a slamming motion during play. Think of them as the demolition derby-style dogs at local dog parks. Their way of delivering a play invitation is to run full speed into other dogs and try to knock them off their feet. Bully breeds find this kind of play fun; other dogs—unsure of how to interpret this rough romping—may find it invasive and painful.

Certain dogs intentionally body slam to be pushy. These dogs may pick on a submissive dog—one that they know they can literally push around at the park—to show others their desire to be the top dog.

 **VET'S NOTE**

> *Excessive rough play can cause torn muscles and even broken legs to the recipient of powerful body slams. Surgery will be necessary to repair the damage and the injured dog may suffer from limited mobility.*

 **HOW TO RESPOND**

Know when to intervene. What may start off as a play maneuver can rapidly escalate into a dangerous display of dominance, or even worse, aggression. If a dog consistently behaves rudely and roughly in a play group, remove him until his inappropriate behavior has been successfully addressed.

Set your dog up for success by selecting canine playmates with play styles that match your dog's. Let body-slamming types play roughhouse and let playmates take turns being the chaser and the chased. For the safety of your dog, do not let a body-slamming dog force play with your senior dog who has arthritis or joint issues, or with a toy breed, such as a Chihuahua.

Dogs who are allowed to body slam without regard for the welfare of their canine playmates may try the same maneuvers on people. These dogs need to be trained in dog obedience and to sharpen their socialization skills among both dogs and humans.

BEHAVIOR TYPES: **Aggressive** *p.178* • **Attention-seeking** *p.179* • **Confident** *p.180* • **Dominant** *p.181* • **Playful** *p.183*

# 70 Leaning Stiffly Forward

○ **On a walk, your dog leans forward on his front legs as he watches another dog approach.**

○ **Your dog stands on his front tiptoes whenever he sees the delivery truck go by.**

## BREEDS

- Akita
- Alaskan Malamute
- Boxer
- Bull Terrier
- Doberman Pinscher
- German Shepherd
- German Shorthaired Pointer

## VET'S NOTE

❯ *Keep a close watch on your dog if he makes this tiptoe action. He is likely preparing to fight, which can result in serious injury to both dogs.*

## WHAT YOUR DOG WANTS

A dog who stands stiffly on his front paws—almost as if he's on his tiptoes—is getting ready to launch an attack. Dogs who assume this position are typically dominant dogs who are prepared to fight to protect their territory. They may also be ready to fight to protect the human at the end of their leash.

By standing stiffly on his front paws, your dog makes himself look larger and more frightening to another dog or threatening human. This action also enables the dog to quickly lunge forward.

## HOW TO RESPOND

If your dog starts making this body language, be alert because a fight is about to ensue. If you are on a walk, keep a tight hold of your dog's leash and give the other dog a wide berth so that your dog cannot lunge at him and make contact.

BEHAVIOR TYPES: **Aggressive** *p.178* • **Confident** *p.180* • **Dominant** *p.181*

# 71 Sharing a Bed

- You may have four dog beds in the house, but there always seems to be a mutual favorite your dogs want to share at the exact same time.

- Two bonded dogs enjoy spooning canine-style in the same dog bed.

- On cold nights, cuddling chums generate heat like a natural furnace.

## BREEDS

- This action is not limited to specific breeds.

## VET'S NOTE

> Dogs recovering from a serious illness or surgery need to have their own bed during this period. Dogs, like people, do their best healing when they rest and are able to sleep uninterrupted.

## WHAT YOUR DOG WANTS

Remember the classic Disney movie *Lady and the Tramp*, with the two dogs who shared the same spaghetti noodle? That is pure canine love—and so is sharing a bed.

Dogs are pack animals. A dog instinctively feels safe and secure when another trusted dog literally has his back at night. Together, they can team up against any real or perceived nighttime threat.

## HOW TO RESPOND

When a dog returns from an overnight stay at a vet clinic or boarding kennel, he can smell like an uninvited stranger to the dog who remained home, and a spat may occur. Prevent this from happening by taking a slightly damp hand towel and rubbing it back and forth over each dog, so they share scents and will happily share a bed again.

# 72 Stealing Treats and Toys

○ **At the local dog park, your dog swipes balls and toys that belong to other dogs.**

○ **The second you drop that squeaky toy, your sneaky dog swoops in for a grab-and-dash.**

## BREEDS

• **This action is not limited to specific breeds.**

## VET'S NOTE

❯ *Your selfish dog may try to swipe a toy or treat from the wrong canine and suffer bite wounds that need to be treated by a vet.*

## ? WHAT YOUR DOG WANTS

Puppies and young dogs who have not aced dog-etiquette rules may be stuck in a "mine-mine-all-mine" mentality. They are clueless about the needs and wants of others.

Some dogs love amassing objects. The more toys and treats these dogs can squirrel away in their dog bed or their secret location in a bedroom closet, the greater their sense of accomplishment.

## ✓ HOW TO RESPOND

Your dog needs a refresher course in the art of sharing, to put the brakes on his canine crime spree. Key vocabulary words for your dog to clearly heed are "drop it," "leave it," and "stay." "Leave it" means do not pick up what does not belong to you; "drop it" means spit it out—now; and "stay" means shift gear into park and stop patrolling the house, neighborhood, playground, and other locations with the intent to steal.

Separate your dogs when you dole out treats. Store highly desirable toys and only bring them out when you can supervise play.

BEHAVIOR TYPES: **Attention-seeking** *p.179* • **Confident** *p.180* • **Dominant** *p.181* • **Playful** *p.183*

# 73 Barking from the House

○ Your dog may be saying to the leashed dog walking past on the sidewalk, "Hey, buster, who gave you permission to be on my turf?"

○ Curtains hanging in your living-room window are no match for a dog barking, lunging, and pawing at the window pane.

## BREEDS

- Australian Shepherd
- Fox Terrier
- German Shepherd
- Miniature Schnauzer
- Scottish Terrier
- West Highland White Terrier

 **WHAT YOUR DOG WANTS**

This can be a bluff bark from dogs who clearly know they are smaller or weaker than the Rottweiler parading past outside. These dogs know that outside dogs cannot get them, thanks to the thick window glass, and the barking makes them feel tough for a few seconds.

Other dogs do not know that the property line ends at the start of the sidewalk and have territorial issues. Strangely, some dogs release aggressive barking at their dog pals while inside the house but are sweet and playful when they greet them face-to-face.

 **HOW TO RESPOND**

Limit your dog's access to the living room so that he cannot unleash his barking barrage.

Teach your dog the "quiet" cue. Reward him when he is silent with grade-A level treats and ignore him when he engages in nuisance barking. Your dog will soon learn which behavior reaps the desired rewards.

 **VET'S NOTE**

> *No specific medical advice for this action.*

BEHAVIOR TYPES: **Aggressive** *p.178* • **Anxious/Stressed** *p.179* • **Bored** *p.180* • **Confident** *p.180* • **Dominant** *p.181* • **Fearful** *p.182*

# 74 Blocking Doorways

○ Your quivering Collie sees you heading out with suitcase in hand and plants herself at the front door to stop you from leaving.

○ Your Rottweiler dares you to try to scoot past her in the doorway.

### BREEDS

• This action is not limited to specific breeds.

### VET'S NOTE

❯ Dogs who hold vigil by the door they use for bathroom breaks may have a urinary tract infection that needs vet care.

 **WHAT YOUR DOG WANTS**

Dogs learn that certain doors have different meanings. The front door may signal that a leashed walk is seconds away. The back door is the entry to the canine bathroom. The door leading to the garage may mean a car ride.

Dominant dogs stubbornly declare what they want by blocking doorways. They know that you cannot simply slip past and ignore them.

Overly anxious or needy dogs park themselves in doorways because they cannot bear to see you leave them alone in the house. Again. Sigh.

Dogs usually block the back door because they need to go outside to the bathroom and they lack thumbs to open the door themselves.

 **HOW TO RESPOND**

Retrain your furry door-blocker to sit on her dog bed or the rug when you leave the house by telling her to "find your spot" and tossing a treat in that direction.

Alternatively, you can put her in a room that is closed off by a dog gate when you are ready to leave.

BEHAVIOR TYPES: **Aggressive** p.178 • **Anxious/Stressed** p.179 • **Attention-seeking** p.179 • **Dominant** p.181 • **Fearful** p.182 • **Sad** p.184

# 75 Leaning against Your Body

- When you watch TV, your dog snuggles you with all her might.

- When your dog sees a stranger, she pushes up against you.

- Your pants are always covered in your Samoyed's hair.

## BREEDS

- American Eskimo Dog
- German Shepherd
- Golden Retriever
- Italian Greyhound
- Labrador Retriever
- Rottweiler
- Samoyed
- Whippet

### ? WHAT YOUR DOG WANTS

Dogs lean on people for different reasons. If your dog leans against you when you pet her, the action is a sign of affection. If she leans in when she gets nervous, she is looking to you for protection. If she leans on you and raises her hackles when someone approaches, she is trying to protect you. However, if she leans against you to keep you from moving, she has a dominance issue that should be addressed.

### ✓ HOW TO RESPOND

The way you handle your dog's leaning will depend on the reason why she is doing it. Obedience training can be the key to solving a dog's leaning when it is related to insecurity or dominance issues. With training, your dog will become more secure and learn that you are the leader.

### VET'S NOTE

> Dogs who start leaning all of a sudden, when they never showed this behavior before, may be feeling sick.

BEHAVIOR TYPES: **Affectionate** *p.178* • **Anxious/Stressed** *p.179*
• **Attention-seeking** *p.179* • **Dominant** *p.181* • **Fearful** *p.182*

# 76 Licking Your Face

o Your Yorkie likes to jump into your lap and slobber all over your chin.

o You have to keep your dog locked up in a back bedroom when you have company because she wants to give everyone a tongue bath.

o You are always washing your face because you are covered with dog spit.

o You have grown tired of fending off your Labrador Retriever's unwanted kisses.

## WHAT YOUR DOG WANTS

When a dog licks your face, she is trying to let you know that she sees you as dominant over her. In the wild, wolves lick the faces of pack members with a higher social standing. Face licking is your dog's way of saying, "I see you as the boss and I want you to accept me and help me. I am not a threat."

By expressing this sentiment, she is prompting you to feed her and take care of her, just like a mother dog or dominant pack member would do for her in the wild.

Puppies are also big face lickers. Your dog's ancestors used to feed their puppies by regurgitating semidigested food for them after the hunt. By licking their mother's face, the puppies triggered her regurgitating reflex. Although modern dogs do not seem to retain this reflex, puppies still have the instinct to lick the faces of both adult dogs and people.

Puppies also use face licking to say, "I am a puppy, small and helpless. I am not a threat to you, so please do not hurt me."

 ## HOW TO RESPOND

Although your dog is trying to tell you something positive when she licks your face, you may not appreciate the slobber-filled gesture. Most people do not enjoy having their face licked by a dog because they think it is unsanitary. Plus, it is just downright messy, especially if your dog strategically and swiftly maneuvers her tongue up your nostrils and in your mouth.

Because face licking is such a strong instinct for dogs, it is difficult to eliminate it completely as a behavior. But you are able to clearly let your dog know that you do not appreciate her actions. End your petting session with your dog, stand up, and leave immediately if she starts going for your face with her tongue. This will definitely reduce her attempts to lick you, since licking your face will not get her the reaction that she intended.

## VET'S NOTE

> If you notice that your dog has bad breath, take her to the vet for a checkup. She may have gum disease or an infected tooth.

## BREEDS

- Golden Retriever
- Labrador Retriever
- Rat Terrier
- Shetland Sheepdog
- Toy Poodle
- Yorkshire Terrier

BEHAVIOR TYPES: Affectionate *p.178* • Attention-seeking *p.179* • Happy *p.182* • Submissive *p.185*

# 77 Mouthing Your Hands

- Your puppy always tries to gnaw on your hand.

- You are growing tired of feeling your puppy's tiny, needle-like teeth on your skin.

- Your Golden Retriever sits by your side when you are watching TV, holding your hand in her mouth.

- Guests do not like to interact with your dog because she slobbers all over their hands.

## BREEDS

- Border Collie
- Cardigan Welsh Corgi
- English Springer Spaniel
- Golden Retriever
- Staffordshire Bull Terrier

## ? WHAT YOUR DOG WANTS

Dogs mouth as a natural behavior when they want your attention or if they want to play. Mouthing is a dog's way of communicating, "Hey, look at me!" This method of getting attention usually works, which reinforces the dog's behavior and convinces her to keep it up.

Since dogs do not have hands, they use their mouths to grasp things. When your dog gently takes your hand into her mouth, she is trying to engage with you. Although it may not seem obvious, this is often an affectionate gesture.

Young dogs also like to mouth hands as a form of playing. When dogs play, they use their mouths to grab each other and, when doing so, they use an inhibited bite so that they do not hurt their playmates. Puppies try to play with humans in the same way, and hands are obvious targets. Dogs tend to focus on a person's hands because you use them for petting.

## VET'S NOTE

> *Mouthing is not dangerous to your dog's health, although it can be dangerous to yours if you accidentally get bitten.*

## ✓ HOW TO RESPOND

While a dog does not mean any harm by mouthing your hands, this is still a behavior that should be discouraged. Not only is it annoying; it can be dangerous. A dog can accidentally bite a hand while playing. Puppies, in particular, have sharp teeth that can really hurt if the dog mouths too hard.

Some trainers believe that a dog should never be allowed to have her teeth touch human skin. This is part of the dog's training not to bite people. They reason that if a puppy learns that it is never okay for her to put her teeth on a human being, she is less likely to resort to biting when she grows up.

To break your dog of the habit of mouthing your hands, offer her a substitute object. A chew toy is always a good alternative to human hands, and most dogs— especially puppies—will gladly take the toy and bite on that instead of you. If your dog refuses to bite on the toy and insists on mouthing your hands, end your interactions with her and walk away. If you do this consistently, she will learn that mouthing gets her nowhere.

# 78 Nipping

○ Your Corgi nips at your child's ankles when they play in the backyard.

○ When you try to move your dog off the couch, she nips at you.

    ○ Your puppy nips at your face when you try to pet her.

    ○ When your toddler pulls your dog's tail, the dog turns around and nips your child.

## BREEDS

- Australian Cattle Dog
- Cardigan Welsh Corgi
- Chihuahua
- German Pinscher
- Jack (Parson) Russell Terrier
- Lhasa Apso
- Pembroke Welsh Corgi

## WHAT YOUR DOG WANTS

## HOW TO RESPOND

Young puppies nip when they play. Puppies understand that a nip is part of the sport of tussling with their siblings or another puppy. When they leave the litter and go to a new home, a puppy usually brings this habit with her. Unfortunately, puppies often extend this type of play to humans.

Adult dogs use nips as warnings, to send the message that they are dominant or that they want you to stop whatever you are doing because they are hurt or feel afraid.

Dogs who nip because they think they make the rules are the most dangerous nippers of all. If you want to move your dog from the couch or bed and she nips at you, she is telling you, "I am in charge, and I say back off."

Some dogs nip because they have an instinct to herd. Dogs who are bred to interact with livestock are naturally nippy because their teeth are a good weapon against stubborn sheep or cattle. For these dogs, nipping is part of their herding style.

Although puppies are being playful when they nip, this action is another one of those unacceptable behaviors that should be discouraged. The best way to do so is to remove yourself from your puppy's presence if she gets nippy. Your dog will soon learn that this action means the end of contact with you.

Herding breeds need to be taught from a young age that they are not allowed to nip at humans. A consistent and firm "No!" and the termination of the play session should be enough to get the message across.

You do not want your dog to call the shots in your household. Pushy, bossy dogs need to learn that you are the leader. The best way to accomplish this is through obedience training.

## VET'S NOTE

> Work with your vet to find a solution. Your dog may require both behavior-modification techniques and calming medication to break this unacceptable behavior.
> Be aware that a dog's nipping can cause serious injury to people.

BEHAVIOR TYPES: **Aggressive** *p.178* • **Dominant** *p.181* • **Fearful** *p.182* • **Playful** *p.183* • **Predatory** *p.184*

# 79 Urinating in Introductions

o   Your brother tells a joke in his booming voice and your fearful dog wets the carpet.

o   Your Cocker Spaniel shows both her awe and admiration for your uncle by piddling during introductions.

o   The driveway has a wet circle seconds after your tall postal carrier leaned over to pet your shy Cavalier King Charles Spaniel.

o   Better stock up on cleaning materials if you know you have a piddler for a pet.

## BREEDS

- Cavalier King Charles Spaniel
- Chihuahua
- Cocker Spaniel
- Dachshund
- English Bulldog

## WHAT YOUR DOG WANTS

Urinating when meeting people is something a fearful dog cannot control. Meeting people can literally scare the pee out of a submissive dog. Cocker Spaniels top the list of breeds that are more prone to weak bladders during meet-and-greets.

Young puppies do not have the muscles to hold their urine and pee when they get excited. Most dogs outgrow this problem.

A person's size, posture (leaning over or rushing up to greet the dog), loud voice, wild gestures, or mood (stern or angry) can trigger submissive urination. In the dog kingdom, this is the universal way to declare that you pose no threat and mean no harm. Loud music, a spat between spouses, or sharp scolding can cause a dog to urinate in an act or expression of complete surrender. Usually, this dog also cowers or quivers.

Dogs who become over-excited when their favorite person returns home or enters a room may also "shower" the floor, as they rush to shower the person with kisses and tail wags.

## VET'S NOTE

> *A bladder infection could cause your dog to uncontrollably urinate.*
> *Some dogs have urinary problems that require surgery or medications to correct.*

## HOW TO RESPOND

The No. 1 rule: do not scold or physically punish a dog who submissively urinates. Such punitive actions will only worsen the situation. Even though you may be frustrated, it is important to clean up the mess without any comment.

Talk to your dog in a calm voice and avoid quick or expressive gestures when you come home, to tone down your dog's exaggerated excitement. Do not say anything and immediately usher your dog outside to go to the bathroom. Only speak in a praising tone when she urinates outside.

Have calm friends properly greet your dog outside. Ask them to crouch down to your dog's level and extend their hand for your leashed dog to sniff. Instruct your friends not to lean over, as this is a threatening gesture in the canine world. Ask them to bend their knees or sit and allow your dog to approach in her own time, to build her confidence. Have the friends then offer your dog a small treat.

Be patient. It takes time for a shy, fearful dog to build up her confidence so that she can experience positive, calm introductions. Eventually, her good introductions will outnumber the bad ones from her past.

BEHAVIOR TYPES: **Anxious/Stressed** *p.179*• **Fearful** *p.182* • **Happy** *p.182* • **Submissive** *p.185*

# 80 Sniffing Guests

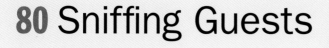

○ Your Siberian Husky strategically positions her long nose at the crotch of your Minister, who is paying you a home visit.

○ A Great Dane only needs one deep sniff to detect what your houseguest recently ate, his mood, and if he happens to own a dog of his own.

○ Your two Yorkies make a beeline for your friend's pant leg and make loud, frequent sniff-sniff-sniff sounds as they circle the leg in unison.

## BREEDS

- American Foxhound
- Basenji
- Beagle
- Bloodhound
- Great Dane
- Norwegian Elkhound
- Rhodesian Ridgeback
- Siberian Husky
- Yorkshire Terrier

## WHAT YOUR DOG WANTS

Dogs do not see sniffing as a bad deed. They are simply performing a natural instinct, which they regard as polite canine etiquette. After all, the canine nose gives the sniffer a wealth of detail about the "sniffee." A dog's nose can catch even the tiniest of scent molecules, download them in her smell receptor, and analyze them quickly. Just like dogs sniff the rear ends of other dogs to gather facts, dogs aim for people's crotches because they harbor more intense scents than other body areas.

Dogs, particularly scent hounds, sniff people to find food and to detect danger or potential threats. They give newcomers the once-over sniff to quickly determine if they are friend or foe.

Some dogs are just pushy. They know no social boundaries and will not think twice about invading a person's personal space during an introduction. These dogs also tend to display bad manners when they greet other dogs for the first time. For example, they charge forward or try to hump the other dog during an introduction.

## HOW TO RESPOND

For a dog who loves to meet everybody and anybody, it is time to rein her in—literally. When a guest rings the doorbell, leash your dog and tether her so she cannot rush up to do her greet-and-sniff routine. Get her to focus on you and heed the "sit" command. The goal is to retrain her to understand that this is the preferred way to say "hello." Reward her with a treat.

Teach your dog to swap sniffing for paw shaking. Start by working with her by yourself. Hold out a treat in your hand positioned just below her nose. Most dogs will paw at the treat. When she does, grab her raised paw, shake it in a friendly way and say, "good paw," then hand over the treat. Next, let her practice with some of your dog-savvy friends.

For stubborn dogs, fill a spray bottle with vinegar and water or mint breath-spray and keep it near the front door. When your dog starts to plunge her nose into a person's crotch, aim and spray. The spray smells unpleasant to most dogs. Do not yell at your dog or spray her in the eyes.

## VET'S NOTE

> *No specific medical advice for this action.*

# 81 Tug-of-war

○ Your Labrador Retriever's grip on the knotted-rope toy is so strong you swear she will pull out her molars.

○ If you aspire to be a major league pitcher, do not risk a shoulder injury by engaging in a game of tug-of-war with your Doberman.

○ You need to head to work, but you cannot resist your dog's charm as she drops the tug toy in your lap and plops into a play bow.

## BREEDS

- American Bulldog
- American Staffordshire Terrier
- Cairn Terrier
- Doberman Pinscher
- Jack (Parson) Russell Terrier
- Labrador Retriever

## WHAT YOUR DOG WANTS

Playing tug-of-war with people is a civilized form of stalking, capturing, and killing prey. It is a game that, when executed properly, provides a healthy outlet for your dog's predatory nature.

Tug-of-war requires your dog to exercise her physical strength and dexterity—as well as using her wits. This is the canine version of a person performing calisthenics while playing a chess match. It is all about sweat and brain power. This challenge is far more popular to most dogs than a simple game of "find the hidden treat."

There are other reasons why your dog may want to play tug-of-war: it can boost her confidence in an appropriate way and it is a terrific outlet for your dog to relieve her stress. During this favorite game, your charged-up dog gets to "kill" prey, win a match, and maybe even revel in a little dog victory dance.

### VET'S NOTE

> *Overzealous dogs may injure their mouths during play. If you notice any blood or loose teeth, take your dog to the vet immediately.*

## HOW TO RESPOND

Set out the rules of tug-of-war to maintain the fact that it is a game in the mind of your dog, and that you, and only you, determine when the game starts and when it finishes.

Select a tug toy that is durable, safe, and size-appropriate for your dog. You do not want a tug toy that can unravel easily or one with sharp edges that can cut her mouth or damage her gums.

Speak in an upbeat, happy tone to start the game. Have your dog get in a "sit," then begin the tugging. Reinforce your dog's "drop it" command during play. Stop the game if she does not drop the toy.

It is totally acceptable to let your dog win tug-of-war more than you do, but you should win at least one-third of the time to maintain your higher status and keep the game engaging to your dog.

Use some game variations by dragging the toy on the ground with a rope for your dog to chase, or toss the tug toy and have your dog retrieve and return it.

BEHAVIOR TYPES: **Attention-seeking** *p.179* • **Bored** *p.180* • **Confident** *p.180* • **Dominant** *p.181* • **Happy** *p.182* • **Playful** *p.183*

# 82 Shadowing

- Your dog quietly follows you from room to room.

- You turn quickly in your kitchen and trip over your Dachshund.

## BREEDS

- Chihuahua
- Dachshund
- English Pointer
- Toy Poodle
- Yorkshire Terrier

 **WHAT YOUR DOG WANTS**

Rescued dogs who have been physically abused regard the person who adopted them as their hero—the one who holds the key to their safety and security. They do not want to lose sight of their owner.

Bored dogs who do not get enough physical or mental exercise tag behind people just to have something to do.

Dogs who lack an iota of confidence and are given constant attention and baby-talk cooing by their owners develop severe separation anxiety.

**VET'S NOTE**

> *If your dog has suddenly become clingy there may be a medical problem, such as gastritis, diabetes, or another condition that needs treatment.*

> *For separation anxiety, your vet may prescribe calming medication and start a behavior-modification program.*

 **HOW TO RESPOND**

You may like the attention, but nip this behavior in the bud. Cut out the constant attention, the baby talk, and carrying your dog in your arms from room to room. These actions only make her more anxious. Ignore her to reduce her Velcro-dog behavior.

Block off the kitchen with a dog gate or put your dog in her crate so you can prepare meals without tripping on her and possibly injuring both of you.

BEHAVIOR TYPES: **Anxious/Stressed** *p.179* • **Attention-seeking** *p.179* • **Bored** *p.180* • **Fearful** *p.182* • **Submissive** *p.185*

# 83 Sitting on Your Feet

○ **When you sit at your desk to answer emails, your dog comes over and sits on your feet.**

○ **You are standing in the kitchen, talking to your spouse, when your dog plants her butt on your feet.**

## BREEDS

- Alaskan Malamute
- Border Collie
- Labrador Retriever
- Rottweiler
- Shih Tzu

## VET'S NOTE

> *If your dog sits on your feet because she wants to be close to you, take this opportunity to give her body the once over, looking carefully for any lumps, bumps, or ticks.*

## WHAT YOUR DOG WANTS

A dog may sit on your feet because she enjoys the physical contact or because she wants to monitor or control your movement.

If your dog is the anxious type who follows you everywhere you go, she is probably sitting on your feet to make sure you do not leave the room without her.

## HOW TO RESPOND

The reason why your dog sits on your feet is important to determine. If your dog is doing it just to be close to you, then learn to appreciate her gesture of affection. You can tell that this is your dog's motive if she is generally an affectionate dog who likes a lot of physical contact with you and other family members.

If you have a dog who shows signs of dominance, the reason for this action may be to keep you from moving. This dog needs obedience training to help her understand that you are the leader.

BEHAVIOR TYPES: Affectionate *p.178* • Anxious/Stressed *p.179* • Attention-seeking *p.179* • Dominant *p.181* • Fearful *p.182*

# 84 Hogging the Bed

○ You cannot get a good night's sleep because your dog keeps pushing you off the bed.

○ If your spouse tries to move your dog over so he can get into bed, he's met with a growl.

○ Your boss just berated you for falling asleep at your desk. You know your pillow-hogging dog is to blame.

## WHAT YOUR DOG WANTS

Dogs consider themselves members of the family, and you as a member of their pack. In the wild, pack mates sleep together, so it makes sense to your dog that everyone in the house should pile into bed together at night, too—including her.

Sleeping with a dog can be great unless that dog is a bed- or pillow-hog. Such dogs sprawl out on the bed and leave little room for humans. Or they plant their heads in the middle of the pillow and force you to sleep with your head on the edge. Try to move one of these dogs and you will get a moan of complaint, an angry growl, or a nasty snap. Even dogs who do not object to being moved may simply return to their original position once you have fallen asleep.

Dogs like to be comfortable when they sleep, just like you do. They will take up as much space as possible so they can spread out and relax.

## HOW TO RESPOND

Some dog trainers discourage allowing your dog to sleep in bed with you because they believe it encourages her to think that she is equal to, or greater, in status than the humans in the pack. These trainers argue that making the dog sleep in her own bed sends the message that she is the subordinate member of the family.

If your dog disturbs your sleep because she takes up too much room on the bed, or she becomes threatening when you try to move her, she needs to sleep in her own bed. Buy her a comfortable bed at a pet supply store and put it close to your bed, so she still feels secure. If she continues to jump up on your bed despite your insistence that she remain on the floor, then crate-train your dog by having her sleep in a crate in your bedroom. She will resist this new arrangement at first, but over time she will get used to it.

## BREEDS

- Bichon Frise
- Dogue de Bordeaux
- Irish Setter
- Labrador Retriever
- Old English Sheepdog
- Standard Poodle

## VET'S NOTE

> *If you sleep with your dog, make sure you maintain a thorough flea-control regimen. The last thing you need is a flea infestation in your bed.*

BEHAVIOR TYPES: **Affectionate** *p.178* • **Confident** *p.180* • **Dominant** *p.181*

# 85 Jumping on People

○ You swear your Jack Russell Terrier has springs for legs by the height she soars just to say hello to Aunt Helen.

○ Your athletic Labrador Retriever keeps a scorecard on the number of houseguests she can knock down.

○ Your girlfriend does not appreciate your Akita leaping up, placing her big paws on her shoulder, and showering her with dog kisses.

## WHAT YOUR DOG WANTS

When dogs are excited, they want to let you know. From a dog's perspective, flinging her body at you with full force is a great way to show it. Unfortunately, jumping up on people is not only annoying; it can be dangerous. Children and the elderly are most at risk—without meaning to, a large dog can knock them to the ground.

Small dogs are especially guilty of jumping up on people. Their goal is to get as close to your face as possible—probably to lick it. From their viewpoint, the best way to do this is to jump up on you. It is tempting to let a small dog jump up because these diminutive canines cannot do much harm. They can scratch legs, however, and ruin stockings. Plus, having a dog throwing herself at you is just plain annoying.

Jumping up is a sure-fire way for your dog to get attention. It is hard to ignore a large, excited dog who is hurtling herself at you.

## BREEDS

- Akita
- Bichon Frise
- Boxer
- Chihuahua
- Dachshund
- Jack (Parson) Russell Terrier
- Labrador Retriever
- Miniature Schnauzer
- Pembroke Welsh Corgi
- Standard Poodle

 ## HOW TO RESPOND

Curb the leaping by teaching your dog to obey the "off" and "sit" commands.

Put a head-type collar on your dog and attach her to a leash that is 6 feet (1.8 m) or longer. Then ask one of your friends to come inside and to ignore your dog—no eye contact, no words. When your dog readies to launch herself and say hello, firmly turn the leash so that your dog must turn her head toward you. Firmly say "off!" When your dog stops trying to jump up, and she sits down, immediately mark that desired behavior by saying "good sit" and giving her a treat.

Practice this with your dog a few times each day to teach her the proper—and polite—greeting etiquette.

## VET'S NOTE

> Take care when you are training your dog not to jump on people. Avoid pushing her off with force, as you can accidentally hurt her and cause a limb injury if she falls.

BEHAVIOR TYPES: Affectionate p.178 • Anxious/Stressed p.179 • Attention-seeking p.179 • Confident p.180 • Dominant p.181 • Happy p.182

# 86 Herding

○ You want to go into the living room to watch your favorite sitcom, but your Border Collie persistently noses you into the kitchen toward her food bowl.

○ Your indoor cat sneaks out the door that has been left ajar, but your Corgi steers the cat back inside and triumphantly barks her success.

○ Ouch! You cannot stop your young Australian Shepherd from nipping at your ankles during a run together.

## BREEDS

- Australian Shepherd
- Belgian Sheepdog
- Border Collie
- Briad
- Canaan Dog
- Entlebucher Mountain Dog
- Norwegian Buhund
- Old English Sheepdog
- Pembroke Welsh Corgi
- Puli
- Shetland Sheepdog
- Swedish Vallhund

## WHAT YOUR DOG WANTS

Some dogs are just genetically hardwired to herd people, farm animals, dogs, cats, and even inanimate objects from point A to point B. The American Kennel Club recognizes 25 herding breeds, ranging from the oversized Old English Sheepdog to the diminutive but determined Pembroke Welsh Corgi. Herding dogs rival all other dogs in their ability to drive cows and other animals many times their size into a specific location, simply by leaping and nipping at their heels.

While many family dogs do not get the chance to herd sheep or cattle, their instinct to herd remains strong. These are smart dogs who want others to play by the rules, their rules, which means staying where a herding dog thinks you should be. If not, herding dogs will bark, nudge with their noses, use their bodies, and even nip, if necessary. Some cannot resist chasing moving people, including happy children who are playing and running.

Certain dogs become obsessed with fetching and chasing objects, such as soccer or tennis balls. They run, fetch, and herd until they collapse in exhaustion.

## VET'S NOTE

> *Herding dogs can overexert themselves and suffer from heat exhaustion.*
> *They can also become overzealous and bite other dogs, which may cause wounds that need to be treated by a vet.*

## HOW TO RESPOND

Herding dogs need a smart leader who they can respect and follow: you. To prevent your herding dog from accidentally causing you or a child to trip and fall, or be nipped, you need to provide her with structured play and discipline.

For starters, crate-train your dog. Put her in a crate with a treat or a toy and let her stay there while your young children run and play in the backyard. Let your dog out of her crate when the children are doing a more sedate activity, such as coloring or reading a book.

To channel your dog's high energy drive, spend 10–15 minutes each day having her herd acceptable objects in an enclosed area. Start and stop the game so she elevates her respect for you. Or enroll her in a herding program so she can channel her natural instincts in an appropriate place.

BEHAVIOR TYPES: **Attention-seeking** *p.179* • **Confident** *p.180* • **Dominant** *p.181* • **Playful** *p.183*

# 87 Stopping during Walks

○ **Must your dog stop, sniff, and inspect every tree and fire hydrant on your block?**

○ **Your dog puts on the brakes without warning and you fall over during a run.**

## BREEDS

- American Bulldog
- Basset Hound
- Coonhound
- German Shorthaired Pointer
- Labrador Retreiver
- Staffordshire Bull Terrier

## VET'S NOTE

❯ *No specific medical advice for this action.*

## ? WHAT YOUR DOG WANTS

To you, the walk has a single mission: to get your dog to do her business, then hustle home. But to your dog, it means taking in as many sights, sounds, and smells as possible, for as long as possible.

Some dogs stop abruptly because they have just discovered an amazing find, such as day-old urine left on a tree by their canine neighbor, Brutus the Bulldog.

Others stop out of fear when a car or skateboard whizzes by, or when an aggressive dog approaches. Certain dogs are just plain fatigued and are too old, too arthritic, or too tired to take another step.

## ✓ HOW TO RESPOND

Investigate your surroundings to determine why your dog is acting like a stop sign. If she is afraid of certain noises, have her get in the "parked" position for a minute or so, then try to lure her back on her feet with a treat.

Pay attention to your dog's gait. Older, arthritic, or taxed dogs will shift their weight, slow down, and may pant heavily. Do not force your dog to cover more distance than necessary.

BEHAVIOR TYPES: **Anxious/Stressed** *p.179* • **Curious** *p.181* • **Dominant** *p.181* • **Predatory** *p.184* • **Sexual** *p.185*

# 88 Mouthing Leash on Walks

○ **Your dog strolls you down the street—leash in mouth.**

○ **Your puppy will not stop gnawing on her new leather leash.**

○ **When you clip on her leash, your dog bites at it like it is a snake.**

## BREEDS

- American Staffordshire Terrier
- Border Collie
- Bull Terrier
- Cocker Spaniel
- Golden Retriever
- Labrador Retriever
- Miniature Pinscher

## VET'S NOTE

> *Repeated leash chewing can weaken the leather or nylon, causing it to break when your dog puts pressure on it. This is potentially dangerous, as she could end up loose in traffic.*

## ? WHAT YOUR DOG WANTS

A teething puppy will chew on just about anything. She is being playful and thinks the leash is a teething toy.

An older dog may mouth the leash as a way to test her position in the pack. If she is not convinced you are the leader, she may be challenging your direction. Dogs with this attitude view the leash as an extension of your hand. They mouth the leash to try to take control from their handler.

## ✓ HOW TO RESPOND

Give your puppy a chilled, hollow-rubber chew toy to ease her teething gums for 30 minutes before your walk. This will tire out her jaw muscles.

Spray cayenne pepper or other flavors that dogs hate on the leash to discourage chewing.

Enroll in an obedience class to teach your dog how to walk in a "heel" position.

Consider selecting a metal chain leash with a soft-grip handle to deter her chewing ways.

# 89 Nosing You Awake

- Your Irish Setter has a bad case of the 2 AM munchies.

- Your ten-week-old puppy uses her cold nose as a wake-up call.

- Your dog just found a tennis ball and it is time for midnight fetch.

## WHAT YOUR DOG WANTS

Puppies less than five months old have small, weak bladders that usually cannot last seven or eight hours without a potty break. They turn to their two-legged leader—you—to usher them outside.

Your house-trained adult dog may have an upset stomach from eating the wrong food or wolfing down dinner too quickly, and does not want to soil indoors. She needs your help to get out to the backyard.

Dogs who love fetch and fail to get enough exercise may want to play day and night—who needs sleep?

## HOW TO RESPOND

Get your dog on a regular bathroom schedule. Avoid feeding her a heavy meal or allowing your dog to drink a lot of water after 7 PM.

Transition your dog to sleeping in a crate if she is obsessed with fetching. Exercise her for 30 minutes before bedtime and give her a chew toy in her crate.

## BREEDS

- Australian Shepherd
- Border Collie
- Irish Setter
- Labrador Retriever
- Standard Poodle

## VET'S NOTE

> *A dog who urinates in the middle of the night may have a urinary tract infection that needs medication.*

BEHAVIOR TYPES: Affectionate *p.178* • Anxious/Stressed *p.179* • Attention-seeking *p.179* • Bored *p.180* • Playful *p.183*

# 90 Pawing People

○ You just sat down to relax and your dog starts pawing at you.

○ Your excited, hungry dog claws at your calves in the kitchen.

○ You put on your pantyhose in the car because you are tired of your dog's pawing ruining them.

### BREEDS

- Australian Shepherd
- Bernese Mountain Dog
- Bichon Frise
- German Shorthaired Pointer
- Labrador Retriever
- Maltese
- Manchester Terrier
- West Highland White Terrier

### WHAT YOUR DOG WANTS

Dogs paw for attention. Your dog may want something to eat or to be petted, or she may be asking you for a game of fetch or to go outside.

Toy breeds are especially good at using their small size and charm to get people to do what they want.

Pawing implies that your dog considers herself dominant—she thinks she can tell you what to do.

### HOW TO RESPOND

Do not respond when your dog paws at you. Instead, ask her to "sit." When all four feet are on the floor tell her she is a good girl, then give her a treat or take her outside to play.

If your small dog demands attention, stand up and walk away. Do not say anything or look at her. When she is quiet, reward her with a cue, such as "good quiet."

### VET'S NOTE

> Keep your dog's nails trimmed to prevent her from scratching you when she paws at you. Trim her nails every four to six weeks, or have your vet or professional groomer trim them for you.

---

BEHAVIOR TYPES: **Affectionate** *p.178* • **Anxious/Stressed** *p.179* • **Attention-seeking** *p.179* • **Dominant** *p.181*

# 91 Leash Yanking

- Your dog rarely gets walked because she throws herself against the leash and no one in the family can deal with it.

- When your dog sees another dog or other animal, she pulls so hard on the leash that she almost yanks you off your feet.

- Your children have fallen down trying to walk your dog because she jerks so hard.

**BREEDS**

- Border Collie
- Chihuahua
- Dalmatian
- English Springer Spaniel
- Great Dane
- Labrador Retriever
- Samoyed
- Siberian Husky

## WHAT YOUR DOG WANTS

Dogs who yank against the leash when they are being walked are excited about being outside. They do not spare a thought for the person at the other end of their leash. All they know is that they want to get where they are going as fast as possible.

Some dogs walk leisurely on a leash until they see another dog, a cat, or a squirrel run by. They then lunge forward with such force, in an attempt to make contact, that they practically pull the person at the other end of the leash off his or her feet. These dogs are fueled by a strong predatory drive.

Lack of training is another reason why dogs pull on the leash. They have not learned that the human is their leader, so they try to take charge of the situation.

Sometimes, dogs who do not get enough exercise have so much pent-up energy that they simply cannot control themselves when they finally do get to go outside and stretch their legs. When these dogs are on a walk, the thinking part of their brain shuts off, and all they can do is go, go, go.

## VET'S NOTE

> Dogs who continuously yank against the leash are at risk of trachea damage. Small dogs are particularly susceptible because of their fragile necks.

## HOW TO RESPOND

Dogs who yank on the leash need two things to help them break this habit: more exercise and more training. If your dog is so cooped up that the mere thought of going on a walk makes her go bonkers, then she needs to get out more. Try throwing a ball to her for ten minutes or so before you go on a walk. This will get rid of some of her excess energy before you have to leash her.

Get your dog to school—or take her to redo a basic obedience class. Obedience training does wonders for curbing leash yanking. Your dog will learn proper leash behavior and will stay aware of you while she is on walks. With training, she will see you as the leader and be less likely to try to take control by dragging you down the street. Instead, she will look to you for guidance on where to go and how fast to get there.

# 92 Limping

○ Your attention-seeking Whippet feigns an injury by limping on her left front leg, forgets, and switches her faux-limping to her right front leg.

○ Your Italian Greyhound takes a hairpin turn too sharply and lets out a yelp.

○ You think your dog is insisting that you shake her paw until you see the giant foxtail lodged in her paw pad.

## BREEDS

- Borzoi
- Chihuahua
- Dachshund
- Dalmatian
- Great Dane
- Irish Wolfhound
- Italian Greyhound
- Labrador Retriever
- Manchester Terrier
- Scottish Deerhound
- Whippet

## WHAT YOUR DOG WANTS

Dogs are a mobile marvel to watch. They can coordinate four legs in a fast gait, maneuver up and down stairs, and leap four times their height to snag a flying object. But they are not invincible and their limbs can be injured from overuse, heavy falls, or tripping.

The growth plates in fast-growing puppies, particularly long-limbed breeds, are vulnerable to muscle and tendon tears, as well as bone fractures.

Some clever canines discover that performing a fake limp garners sympathy—and attention. They are not so clever when they switch allegedly injured legs.

Dogs are vulnerable to foot injuries from stepping on burrs, broken glass, rock salt, and other items that bruise or cut paw pads. All can result in lameness.

Long-backed dogs, such as Dachshunds, and big dogs, such as Great Danes and Labrador Retrievers, are at greater risk of hip and elbow dysplasia that impairs their mobility.

## VET'S NOTE

> Do not dismiss limping, as the cause may be torn muscles, ligaments, or tendons. A vet needs to perform a thorough physical examination that goes beyond checking the leg. X-rays may be taken and pain medication prescribed.

> Hip dysplasia, elbow dysplasia, puncture wounds, arthritis, panosteitis (inflammation of long leg bones), or osteosarcoma (bone cancer) are other possible causes of your dog's limp.

## HOW TO RESPOND

Listen to professional dog trainers and be sure not to push your young pup to leap, jump, or climb before her growth plates are formed. Agility is a popular sport, but a responsible dog trainer will not let dogs that are less than six months old enroll, because agility requires dogs to make quick turns, sprint through tunnels, climb A-frames, weave through poles, and leap over hurdles.

Carefully inspect your dog's legs, paws, and in between her toes during and after you take a hike through the woods or a walk on an icy winter's day. Look for foreign bodies lodged in her feet or tenderness to her legs.

Practice exercises that provide strength and flexibility to your dog's hind legs, especially if she is a large dog or has a long back. Have your dog sit up on her hind legs and hold the "begging" pose for five to ten seconds. This will increase the blood flow to her back legs and improve her joint mobility.

BEHAVIOR TYPES: **Attention-seeking** *p.179* • **Curious** *p.181* • **Playful** *p.183*

# 93 Sleeping under Covers

- Your Dachshund tunnels under the covers down to your toes with the agility of a gopher.

- Your dog hates the feel of your bedspread and digs under the sheets to snooze.

## BREEDS

- Chihuahua
- Dachshund
- Doberman Pinscher
- Italian Greyhound
- Mexican Hairless (Xoloitzcuintle)
- Miniature Pinscher
- Rat Terrier
- Vizsla

## VET'S NOTE

> No specific medical advice for this action.

## WHAT YOUR DOG WANTS

Your bed is the place in your home, rivaled only by the sofa, that harbors your strongest scent. Dogs who adore their owners want to be close to them, especially when sleeping. Being able to "spoon" you brings your dog contentment and security in the dark hours.

Some breeds, such as the Mexican Hairless and Italian Greyhound, lack much hair. These dogs need body warmth to keep them from getting cold at night.

Terriers are born diggers, bred to catch gophers and rabbits. Digging under sheets is easy for them.

## HOW TO RESPOND

Relax. Your dog will not suffocate by snoozing under the sheet, blanket, or bedspread. But to get a solid night's sleep, train your dog to sleep under the sheets on the other side of your bed. Or strike a compromise with your small- to medium-sized dog by ushering her into a tunnel dog bed placed on top of your bed.

BEHAVIOR TYPES: **Affectionate** *p.178* • **Anxious/Stressed** *p.179* • **Attention-seeking** *p.179* • **Happy** *p.182*

# 94 Watching Television

○ **Your Poodle cannot take her eyes off the giraffes racing on your high-definition TV screen.**

○ **Your Miniature Schnauzer is convinced that although the dog in the commercial is one-dimensional and lacks a scent, it is very real.**

## BREEDS

- Akita
- Australian Cattle Dog
- Beagle
- Border Collie
- Doberman Pinscher
- Jack (Parson) Russell Terrier
- Miniature Schnauzer
- Norwegian Elkhound
- Poodle
- Samoyed
- Siberian Husky

### VET'S NOTE

❯ *No specific medical advice for this action.*

 **WHAT YOUR DOG WANTS**

Some dogs are curious and more attuned to their surroundings than others. They notice that people stare at a big, flat screen and want to know what is so fascinating. Experts say dogs cannot always tell what an object is on screen, but are intrigued by movements, shapes, and sounds coming from the television. High-definition screens sharpen the focus.

Dogs with high prey drives do not care if the prey is a rabbit in an open field or a car commercial that features an animated talking lizard—there is movement happening and the chase is on!

 **HOW TO RESPOND**

Some highly aroused dogs unleash a barrage of barks, or worse, lunge at or bite the TV in attack. This can injure them and prove costly to you.

If your dog interrupts your favorite show, usher her to a closed room with a keep-busy toy and turn on the radio to mute sounds coming from your TV.

BEHAVIOR TYPES: Anxious/Stressed *p.179* • Curious *p.181* • Dominant *p.181* • Predatory *p.184*

# 95 Bringing Objects

○ Your dog acts like it is your birthday every day by constantly delivering you presents, such as your left slipper and the television remote.

○ You vow to take your dog on a long walk tomorrow, but she drops the leash in your lap and starts her wiggling, pleading ritual.

○ You try to show gratitude, but are disgusted by the decaying fish your dog has plopped at your feet.

## BREEDS

- Beagle
- Cairn Terrier
- Cardigan Welsh Corgi
- Golden Retriever
- Labrador Retriever
- Portuguese Water Dog
- Rottweiler
- Shetland Sheepdog

**WHAT YOUR DOG WANTS**

Most dogs are born pleasers and they want to see you happy. Since they do not have access to car keys or credit cards, they do their own style of shopping by bringing you what they perceive to be items of value.

Dogs who are bored by a lack of play or exercise may turn into delivery dogs, as a way to grab your attention and convince you it is time to play. They bring you the leash when they want to go out on a walk and soak up all the smells, sights, and sounds of your neighborhood. Or they may drop a drool-dripping tennis ball in your lap to signal it is time for a game of fetch. Think of it as canine currency.

Certain breeds, such as Golden Retrievers, have a long history of using their soft mouth-grips to fetch ducks and other game back to hunters without marring prey with bite marks. Even though your dog may have never participated in an actual hunt, the instinct is part of her DNA. She is simply following in the paw steps of her ancestors—in today's latest style, of course.

 **VET'S NOTE**

› *If your dog picks up a poisonous plant, a bottle containing pool chemicals, or other hazardous substance, she may need to have a vet induce vomiting and provide her with subcutaneous fluids to recover.*

 **HOW TO RESPOND**

Refocus your dog's drive to bring you objects by making this an educational game. Expand her vocabulary by having her learn to bring you specific objects, such as her red ball, her monkey-shaped squeaker toy, or her leash. Or stash one of her favorite toys out of sight and have your dog use her sense of smell to sniff out its hiding place and bring it to you. Watch as your dog's eyes light up in excitement and her confidence builds when she brings you the item you requested.

Become a tidy housekeeper. Place high-temptation items, such as the television remote, your slippers, and other objects that you do not want covered in slobber or sporting teeth marks, out of paw's reach.

Have your dog "sit" or do another cue before leashing her up for a walk. She needs to view you as the benevolent leader, the person in charge.

# 96 Begging for Your Food

o Your dog wins a seat at the dinner table after wearing you down with her begging, brown eyes.

o Your dog has more waddle than wiggle, and overeating is to blame.

o Your dog looks at the dry kibble in her bowl, yawns, and tries to help you in the kitchen at dinnertime.

## BREEDS

- Bull Mastiff
- English Springer Spaniel
- Flat-coated Retriever
- German Shepherd
- Golden Retriever
- Labrador Retriever
- Scottish Terrier
- Standard Poodle
- West Highland White Terrier

## WHAT YOUR DOG WANTS

When our ancestors domesticated dogs, the ever-alert canine quickly associated people with being a reliable food source. Dogs are pack animals and play by a social hierarchy. Top dogs always eat before lower-ranking dogs.

Most dogs are born chowhounds and never pass up the chance for seconds, or even better, people food. Bacon, roast beef, scrambled eggs, and salmon make a dog's mouth water with delight because of the high protein content and beckoning aromas. Frankly, some dry kibble is boring and tasteless to certain dogs.

There is a powerful food connection between people and their pets. We like to reward dogs for good behavior with treats. We sneak them a piece of food from our plate and before you know it, a bad habit has been created. Unchecked, this action can escalate to people becoming food-dispensing machines for their dogs. Some dogs start to paw and even growl at you to hand over food from your plate—an act of dominance.

## VET'S NOTE

›  *Work with your vet to select a quality brand of dog food that best matches your dog's age, activity level, breed, and health status.*

›  *Sadly, more than one-third of dogs are overweight, or worse, obese. The extra pounds make these dogs candidates for a host of health woes, including diabetes, arthritis, heart conditions, hip dysplasia, pancreatitis, and more.*

## HOW TO RESPOND

If you truly want to ensure that your dog enjoys a long, healthy life and you spend your money at the vet clinic wisely, then put the brakes on food begging. Feed your dog two or three meals a day and carefully measure out each portion so that you do not overfeed her.

Feed your dog in a different room, one with a door you can close, while you enjoy your meal without the constant glare of begging eyes or the sounds of her soft whimpers.

If you want to give your dog something from your plate, wait until after your meal. Save a piece of meat, minus the fat and gristle, and have your dog display canine table manners by sitting and waiting. Place the meat treat in her bowl and have her heed the "leave it" cue until you say "okay."

BEHAVIOR TYPES: **Attention-seeking** *p.179* • **Dominant** *p.181* • **Predatory** *p.184*

# 97 Sensitive Toes

○ Your Shih Tzu snaps at you when you try
to examine in between her toes.

○ Your dog has to have
her toenails trimmed
by a vet because a
sedative is required.

○ Your dog snatches her
feet away if you touch
them when petting her.

## BREEDS

- Australian Cattle Dog
- Boston Terrier
- Bull Terrier
- Dalmatian
- Papillon
- Pembroke
  Welsh Corgi
- Shih Tzu

## WHAT YOUR DOG WANTS

Just as with humans, dogs are more protective over certain areas of their bodies. The dog's foot is one of those sensitive areas that many dogs prefer not to be touched.

If your dog does not want you to touch her feet, she will snap, growl, or yank her foot away. These actions are all her way of sending one clear message: "My feet are off-limits. Stop messing with them."

If a dog has had her toenails trimmed too short, she may associate pain with having her feet handled. Cutting a nail too close to the quick can make it bleed and cause your dog discomfort.

Some dogs are just naturally sensitive about having their paws manipulated, probably because they never had them handled when they were pups. While most parts of your dog's body have been touched in the petting process, the feet may have been sorely neglected.

## VET'S NOTE

> Your dog needs to have her toenails trimmed regularly to maintain healthy paws and legs.
> If your dog's nails are difficult to trim because she will not let you touch her feet, talk to your vet. Until your dog can learn to tolerate foot handling, she may need a sedative at nail-trimming time.

## HOW TO RESPOND

Whether your dog has had a negative experience with having her feet touched or she is just not used to them being handled, you can help fix the problem by using treats to associate paw touching with something positive.

Whenever you touch her feet, give her a healthy treat as a reward. Let her have the treat at the same time as you touch her, so that she makes the connection between food and handling. This method can do wonders to help cure a foot-wary dog. The exception is if your dog tries to bite you when you reach for her foot. If this is the case, you may need to get help from a professional trainer.

Be sure to touch your puppy's feet as often as you can to help her get used to the sensation. With enough touching, she will learn to accept foot handling, which will make it much easier to keep her toenails in good shape.

If your dog has dark-colored nails, you may need the aid of a professional groomer so that you do not accidentally cut the quick and cause the nail to bleed.

BEHAVIOR TYPES: **Anxious/Stressed** p.179 • **Fearful** p.182

# 98 Refusing to Eat from Bowl

- You mix dry kibble and canned food in your dog's bowl, only to have her give it a blank stare and refuse to take one bite.

- Your fussy Miniature Schnauzer does not like to get her beard saturated with pieces of wet kibble.

- Your Pekingese has always had a hardy appetite but now just walks away from a full bowl of food.

- You find yourself getting on your hands and knees to mimic eating, in the hope of kick-starting your dog's appetite.

## BREEDS

- This action is not limited to specific breeds.

## ? WHAT YOUR DOG WANTS

Changes in a dog's routine, such as a new move, the addition of a family pet, or the departure of a beloved family member, can cause her emotional stress and diminish her appetite.

Some dogs know that people food tastes better than their kibble or canned food, and masterfully manipulate their owners to feed them real chicken, cooked carrots, and other foods from their plate. These dogs work on a person's guilt, to their benefit.

Dogs can develop allergies to certain foods, such as lamb or wheat, and may instinctively avoid them.

Other dogs refuse to eat because they do not like the smell of their bowls. Plastic bowls, in particular, can trap bacteria and other foul odors.

## VET'S NOTE

> *Dogs need good nutrition to stay healthy and should not go a couple of days without eating. Loss of appetite can signal a host of medical disorders.*

> *Refusing to eat can also mean that your dog has a dental problem, such as a broken tooth or gingivitis, which is causing her pain. Dogs should have their teeth cleaned by vets regularly to prevent tartar buildup and keep their gums a healthy bubble-gum pink color.*

> *An unbalanced diet can lead to a poor coat, loss of muscle tone, and damage to a dog's organs. Work with your vet to select the right, nutritionally complete diet for your dog.*

##  HOW TO RESPOND

Establish a meal time limit for fussy eaters who do not have any legitimate health issues. Place the food bowl down and pick it up after 15 minutes. Do this a few times to train your dog that you do not operate a 24-hour dog diner.

Try serving your dog's food in a wider bowl, a plate, or on a placemat. Some dogs do not like their whiskers scrunched while eating, or like to peck at their food one kibble at a time.

Replace the plastic food bowl with a stainless steel bowl that has a no-skid bottom. Get into the habit of washing your dog's bowls in hot, soapy water and rinsing them thoroughly to reduce bacteria contamination.

If your dog has a weakened appetite after surgery or another temporary situation, serve her a bland diet comprising cooked rice and boiled chicken until she fully recovers.

BEHAVIOR TYPES: Anxious/Stressed *p.179* • Attention-seeking *p.179* • Bored *p.180* • Sad *p.184*

# 99 Stealing Objects

○ You find your dog carrying around the dirty socks you left in the hamper.

○ Your dog helped herself to the roast you were defrosting on the counter.

○ You spend 20 minutes every night chasing your dog, trying to get your slipper away from her.

○ Your daughter has not seen her favorite stuffed toy for a week.

WHAT YOUR DOG WANTS

When your dog steals something, she wants to take possession of the object for any number of reasons. She may want to play with it, because she views the object as a toy. Clothing, shoes, and children's toys are favorite items for canine kleptomaniacs. These dogs may enjoy chewing up the object, tearing it, or just tossing it around.

When a dog takes something that is not hers, she does not know she is stealing. She simply sees something she wants and goes for the object.

If your dog steals food, her motives are obvious. Even though she may be well fed, your dog may still have the urge to snack on people food. If she does, she will try to take anything you leave on the counter or table that smells good and is within her reach.

Some dogs steal because they long for your attention. They will take something just to prompt you to chase them. These dogs know what is important to you and they will grab the item just at the right time, so you see them do it. Their great hope is that you will follow in hot pursuit.

✓ HOW TO RESPOND

If your dog steals toys, it is best to provide her with her own objects to gnaw on. Until she gets into the habit of playing with her items only, keep your laundry, shoes, and children's toys secure—store them somewhere she cannot reach.

If she steals food, you also need to be vigilant about keeping edibles out of reach.

If it is the chase she is after, stop rewarding her stealing with what she perceives as a game. Instead, teach her to bring the object back to you by calling her and offering her a treat in exchange for the stolen item. Rather than steal your slippers, she may end up bringing them to you in the end.

 BREEDS

- Chesapeake Bay Retriever
- Dogue de Bordeaux
- German Shepherd
- Golden Retriever
- Papillon
- Yorkshire Terrier

 VET'S NOTE

› *If your dog is a chronic food-stealer, talk to your vet about possibly changing her diet to something she will find more satisfying.*
› *Keep your dog from swallowing objects that are not meant for eating. She may develop a blockage in the intestines that can require surgery.*

BEHAVIOR TYPES: Anxious/Stressed *p.179* • Attention-seeking *p.179* • Playful *p.183*

# **100** Fetching

○   Your Border Collie is so fast that it seems only two seconds pass before she is ready for you to fling the flying disc again.

○   Your playful Cairn Terrier noses the tennis ball under the recliner and barks for you to retrieve it. As soon as you relax, she pushes the ball under again.

○   You take your Labrador Retriever to the abandoned dog park after a major snowstorm and feel like you can finally enjoy a walk together—that is, until she plunges her head into a snow bank, fishes out a frozen tennis ball, and insist you play fetch.

**WHAT YOUR DOG WANTS**

To a dog, chasing balls, sticks, or most other airborne toys is not that much different from chasing rabbits and other small prey. Your dog's ancestors were the original eat-on-the-run types. The chase brought them a positive prize—food and a full belly. Modern-day dogs do not need to pursue their meals, but the chase-and-catch instinct is still hard-wired into them, especially in hunting dog breeds. Mild-mannered dogs, such as Afghans, are not big fans of fetching.

Look at your dog's favorite tennis ball with a fresh perspective. When it is full of spit and the ball has gone a bit spongy, it mimics the texture and feel of a downed duck flushed out by a Golden Retriever.

Fetching is a great way for dogs to burn off excess energy and maintain a healthy weight.

 **BREEDS**

- Border Collie
- Cairn Terrier
- Golden Retriever
- Labrador Retriever
- Nova Scotia Duck Tolling Retriever
- Pembroke Welsh Corgi
- Portuguese Water Dog
- Shetland Sheepdog
- Whippet

 **HOW TO RESPOND**

If your dog likes to chase and fetch a toy but does not consistently bring it back to you, it is time to outfox her with the bait-and-switch strategy. Show your dog one of her B-level fetching toys and get her excited. Toss it, and as she picks it up, show her a more favored toy. Pretend that you are going to toss this favorite toy in the opposite direction. She may drop the first to come racing to you to chase the second one. While she does that, pick up the first and repeat this sequence. Before she realizes it, she is coming back to you consistently with a fetch toy. Success!

Make the game more advanced by teaching your dog such commands as "bring it," "give it," and "drop it." These cues also come in handy when your dog accidentally picks up one of your pills or a chocolate cookie. Heeding the "drop it" cue will keep her from getting sick.

Stay in control. Start and stop the game of fetch to prevent your dog from becoming bossy or obsessed.

 **VET'S NOTE**

> *No specific medical advice for this action.*

BEHAVIOR TYPES: **Attention-seeking** *p.179* • **Bored** *p.180* • **Confident** *p.180* • **Dominant** *p.181* • **Obsessive-Compulsive** *p.183* • **Playful** *p.183*

## Affectionate

## Aggressive

Dogs display love and appreciation toward favorite people in a number of different ways. Some common signs a dog uses to show affection are: shadowing; licking your face or hands; wagging her tail in a relaxed side-to-side or circular cadence; rolling over to expose her belly, as a sign of trust or a request for a belly rub; placing her head on your lap; rubbing her body against your legs; making playful yaps; bringing you favorite toys or other items, such as your shoes; nudging your hand with her nose; standing up on her hind feet in front of you; and greeting you with a relaxed open-mouthed grin.

Dogs show affection toward other dogs by sharing their toys, nestling together in a bed during a nap, and engaging in mutual grooming, particularly cleaning one another's ears. In greeting each other, affectionate dogs may leap up and touch front paws, but their bodies are relaxed, not tense.

This term covers the full gamut—from the display of subtle facial expressions and body postures, to snapping and an outright physical attack on another dog, person, or animal during a real or perceived conflict. An aggressive dog displays some or all of these signs: intense and prolonged staring; a tense body; ears forward or pinned back; lips open to expose teeth and a snarl; growls or loud barks; raised hair (hackles) on the back and shoulders; tail held up high and straight; and body leaning forward.

Aggression can be fear-related, territorial, protective of food and other resources, defensive, drug-induced, pain-related to a medical condition or injury, maternal (mother dog being protective of her litter of pups), learned, redirected, predatory, trained (police dogs), and idiopathic (cause unknown). Uncontrolled play, particularly between young dogs, can escalate into aggression that can be denoted by hard bites and physical body slamming. Fear-aggressive dogs are more likely to bite than dominant dogs.

# Anxious/Stressed

Some dogs lack the skills to adjust to new people, dogs, or surroundings and, consequently, they become frustrated, frightened, and confused. Manifestations of anxiety or stress in dogs include lip licking, cowering behind owner, excessive shedding, turning down treats or not eating, avoiding eye contact, sweating through foot pads, quivering, blinking excessively, displaying dilated pupils, panting, whining, vocalizing, pacing, scratching at self, yawning, and clinging to owner. Ears tend to be back and pressed flat against the neck. Eyes tend to look glassy. Tail is tucked under. Some stressed dogs do what is known as submissive urination. In trying to self-calm, a dog may do a body shake that resembles shaking off water even though he is dry.

Resist talking in cooing tones or baby talk, as these vocalizations will only cause the dog to feel more anxious and nervous. Dogs that suffer from extreme anxiety need a combination of calming medications and behavior-modification techniques.

# Attention-seeking

Some dogs are not shy about what they want from you and do whatever it takes to get your attention. They may "bark-bark-bark" in rapid succession, whine, paw at you, or drop toys in your lap. Even though these dogs do not speak English, they clearly convey that they want you to pay attention to them—now! Other signs attention-seeking dogs employ include stealing your sock and running into the other room, tugging at your sweatshirt or pant leg, barking when you are on the telephone, mouthing your hand, licking you, gutting the stuffing out of a toy in front of you, and, in extreme situations, urinating and defecating on the floor.

If you cater immediately to your dog's demands, she will learn to use her manipulative behavior to her advantage and actually train you to heed her wishes. Attention-seeking antics that were cute when your dog was a puppy can escalate into nuisance and destructive behaviors if not properly addressed.

## Bored

Dogs put the "d" in doing, and when they are not given enough mental or physical stimulation they often show their boredom in destructive and unwanted behavior. It is their way of communicating exasperation at ho-hum routines. Imagine spending every day in your house stuck in one room with no TV, computer, or other engaging gadget. Or imagine eating the same meal or taking the same walk, at the same time, for the same duration, every day. You would become bored, too.

Dogs show their displeasure of the mundane by barking excessively, digging in the yard or garden, shredding the toilet paper, chewing curtains, and a laundry list of other misdeeds that are all performed to banish boredom. Providing daily exercise and play, and giving your dog hard-rubber toys stuffed with kibble or cheese are great ways to keep him engaged in positive ways.

## Confident

A confident dog is self-assured and feels safe and content in her surroundings. She stands tall or sits with her head held high. Her eyes are bright and her look is direct but not intense. Her ears are perked up but her mouth is relaxed and slightly open. Her tail moves gently or is hung in a relaxed posture. If lying down, her body is relaxed and she may position herself in the middle of the room rather than in a corner. If she is walking, she moves in a steady, upbeat pace, as if to convey, "Hey, look at me!"

Confident dogs adapt easily to new situations and strange new sounds. However, these dogs fare best when they regard their owners as their benevolent leaders. Confident dogs will not show any fear or back down from dogs who they perceive are displaying threatening actions toward them.

## Curious

Blessed with super senses to see, hear, smell, and taste, curious dogs check out their surroundings by tapping into all their senses—cats do not have the monopoly on this inquisitive behavior. Humans may smell a rump roast in the oven, but curious dogs sniff the air and are able to deduce each and every ingredient. They perk up their ears or turn to catch a novel sound. They cock their heads in concentration when a dog appears on your flat-screen, high-definition television.

Look for their tails to be hoisted and possibly wagging. Curious dogs may stand a bit forward on their front toes and their mouths are usually closed or slightly open with teeth covered. These dogs focus on the object that is garnering their attention, but they will stare without glaring.

## Dominant

Being bossy and pushy are the hallmarks of dominant behavior. Dominance falls somewhere in the middle of the behavior spectrum between confidence and aggressiveness. A dominant dog regards himself as the top dog and, as such, acts outgoing and assertive, rarely apologizing for his behavior or displaying any fear postures. This is the dog who can charm you one minute and can upset you the next by rushing over to a submissive dog, looming over him, and unleashing some "I-mean-business" barks.

The classic dominant posture includes ears up straight or forward, mouth closed or slightly open, eyes wide open, stiff tail raised, nose wrinkled, a tall stance, and is usually accompanied by low growls. Dominance tends to develop in dogs who lack proper obedience training and socialization skills, and who view their owners as lacking leadership qualities. Unchecked, dominant behavior can develop into a more dangerous condition: dominance aggression.

## Fearful

## Happy

Frightened and lacking confidence, fearful dogs take on defensive postures. Look for their ears to be back; their pupils to be dilated; their noses to be wrinkled; their bodies to be low, as if ready to flee; their tails to be low or tucked between their hind legs; their mouths to quiver and possibly release drool; and their eyes to be squinted, avoiding contact, or showing the whites (called whale eye). Look carefully and you will notice these dogs often put most of their weight on their back legs. They may display a grimace, as indicated by the sides of the mouth being pulled back.

Whatever or whomever they are confronting, fearful dogs are frozen in place or desperately looking for escape exits. In full fear, they may respond to kind acts of petting by snapping or nipping because they mistakenly think that you are invading their safety zone.

Oh, to be as joy-filled as a happy pup! Full of glee and delight, a happy dog may even display a smiling mouth, with her muzzle relaxed and her mouth slightly open. The eyes are alert and wide open. Look for the full-body wiggle or the classic "C" curve, in which a happy dog curves his torso in the shape of this letter, usually leaning against your legs. The tails of happy dogs tend to be up or out from the body and wagging in a circular motion. Most happy dogs vocalize by yapping, delivering short, high barks, or making sing-song sounds. Some dogs, particularly small dogs, for reasons that remain unknown, sneeze when they are happy.

# Obsessive-Compulsive

Dogs who spin or chase their tails, frantically pace or circle, chase lights or shadows, bark intensely and rhythmically without cessation, bob their heads, excessively lick to the point of causing bald spots, or attack inanimate objects (such as food bowls) without logical explanation are displaying examples of obsessive-compulsive disorder (OCD) behaviors. These are abnormal actions that can increase to the point where they can potentially cause harm to the dog or others. Sadly, OCD dogs do not seem to be able to find the "off" switch to stop these behaviors on their own.

OCD is not just a behavioral problem—it is a neurological disorder that requires medication and proper behavior modification to try to correct it. Causes include an inability to handle stress or conflict, or changes in the household routine, such as adding a new pet or relocating.

# Playful

People send out invitations via email or on stationary for friends to attend our parties. Dogs do not need computer keyboards or stamps to convey when they want to party like a pup. They plop into the play bow, with their rear ends up in the air, their mouths open, tongues out, and their front legs lowered and stretched out in front. They may pant rapidly to convey pleasure and playfulness, or run up to you and greet you with a wide grin and merrily wagging tail.

Dogs signal playtime with canine chums not only with play bows but also by making high-pitched barks and growls. Some breeds even engage in friendly body slams, but you will notice that their bodies are relaxed and not tense. Appropriate play—with people and other dogs—helps dogs learn proper social skills and provides them with a suitable outlet for any pent-up energy.

## Predatory

All dogs have some degree of predatory drive that kicks in when triggered by a strong stimulus, such as a fleeing squirrel or cat. Whether the dog gives chase or ignores the fast-moving critter depends on his genetics and training. Humans have genetically tweaked some dog breeds to herd cattle or sheep, sniff and flush out hiding game, such as quails, or to burrow through dirt tunnels to fetch squirrels.

Predatory signs include stalking, staring at, or silently pursuing small animals, or giving chase to fast-moving inanimate objects, such as cars or skateboards. The ears tend to be up and forward, the eyes alert and wide open, and the body tense, crouched low, and ready to spring forward. The tail is usually extended straight out from the body and there is little to no vocalization before giving chase, so as not to alert the prey.

## Sad

Dogs are not immune to feeling depressed or from experiencing grief because of the loss of a loved one, including a person or another dog. A dog may get depressed because of changes in lifestyle, such as moving into a new home, or miss a family member now off to college. Dogs are social animals that build friendship bonds and are empathetic—tapping into our feelings.

Signs of sadness that dogs display include sleeping more, losing interest in activities such as walks or playing fetch, eating less, looking at you with quiet eyes and head placed on paws, and inexplicably losing weight. Surprisingly, new research indicates that some dogs also suffer from seasonal affective disorder (SAD) as autumn moves into winter and there is less sunlight available. In cases of SAD, or if a dog suffers severe, prolonged sadness, a vet may prescribe medication to elevate her mood.

# Sexual

# Submissive

The urge to reproduce is strong in dogs because it is essential for the survival of the species. Male puppies as young as five weeks old engage in sexual play by mounting their littermates. Intact males maintain interest in mating, but the drive to mate in unspayed females is seasonal and depends on when they go into heat.

During canine courtship, the male and female may nuzzle, rub under each other's chins, walk parallel to each other, and run together. They may also press heads together.

Prior to copulation, the male may lick the female's genitalia, chase away other male suitors, or be initially rebuffed by the female. The male will mount the female and his penis will swell, causing an erection. The locking of the penis in the vagina is called a copulatory tie. Surprisingly, in this position, the pair can fend off competing suitors. After mating, the pair will lick and groom each other, then repeat the act of copulation.

A submissive dog uses her entire body to valiantly convey that she comes in peace and poses absolutely no threat when confronted by a dominant or aggressive dog, or imposing person. With ears down and flat against her head and her eyes narrowed and avoiding direct contact, the dog is in a subordinate pose. She may attempt to lick or nuzzle the other dog's muzzle or a person's face in a show of deference and respect.

Certain submissive dogs lift a front paw—perhaps the canine version of waving the white flag of surrender. Some dogs lie down and expose their bellies and others may shift their body weight back and forth. Extremely submissive dogs will dribble a bit of urine during confrontations. Their tails are usually tucked under and the only sounds they make, if any, tend to be soft whimpers or whines.

# Index

# Acknowledgments

Author Arden Moore wishes to thank dog expert and friend Audrey Pavia; her sister, Debra Moore; and, of course, her cool canines Chipper and Cleo, for their support in helping her produce this, her 24th pet book.

The publisher wishes to thank Deonie Fiford and Athena Chambers for their contributions to this publication.

**Please note**: always consult a vet before you treat your dog. Advice in Vet's Notes is generic in nature and as dogs are individuals, they may exhibit behaviors for reasons not mentioned in this book, and require alternative or additional medical treatments. Also, Breeds boxes list breeds that most commonly exhibit each behavior and are not exhaustive.

## PICTURE CREDITS

b = bottom, l = left, r = right, t = top

AL = Alamy
BS = Bigstock
CB = Corbis
DT = Dreamstime
GI = Getty Images
IS = iStockphoto
SH = Shutterstock
TS = Thinkstock

1 SH; 2 SH; 5 SH; 6–7 DT; 8 DT; 10–11 DT; 12 TS; 14 IS; 16 AL; 18 DT; 19 IS; 20 CB; 22 SH; 24 AL; 26 BS; 28 IS; 30 GI; 32 GI; 33 IS; 34 TS; 36 BS; 38 GI; 39 IS; 40 IS; 42 CB; 44 IS; 46 BS; 47 CB; 48 SH; 50 BS; 51 SH; 52 SH; 54 BS; 56 DT; 58 IS; 60 BS; 61 BS; 62 IS; 64 DT; 66 BS; 68 IS; 70 IS;

72 IS; 74 IS; 76 SH; 78 GI; 80 IS; 82 DT; 84 AL; 86 AL; 88 GI; 90 IS; 92 BS; 94 AL; 96 IS; 98 IS; 100 IS; 102 GI; 104 SH; 105 IS; 106 SH; 108 GI; 110 SH; 111 IS; 112 GI; 114 DT; 115 GI; 116 DT; 118 BS; 119 DT; 120 CB; 122 SH; 124 GI; 126 SH; 128 DT; 130 GI; 131 GI; 132 AL; 133 AL; 134 BS; 135 AL; 136 TS; 138 SH; 140 GI; 142 AL; 144 AL; 146 GI; 148 AL; 149 AL; 150 SH; 152 GI; 154 AL; 156 CB; 157 GI; 158 GI; 159 BS; 160 CB; 162 SH; 164 GI; 165 GI; 166 IS; 168 GI; 170 GI; 172 BS; 174 TS; 176 IS; 178l TS; 178r SH; 179l TS; 179r IS; 180l IS; 180r BS; 181l SH; 181r IS; 182l IS; 182r SH; 183l SH; 183r SH; 184l IS; 184r SH; 185l GI; 185r SH; 186b SH; 186t SH; 187 DT; 188 SH; 189b DT; 189t SH; 190b DT; 190t IS; 191 SH; 192 SH.